hot *textiles*

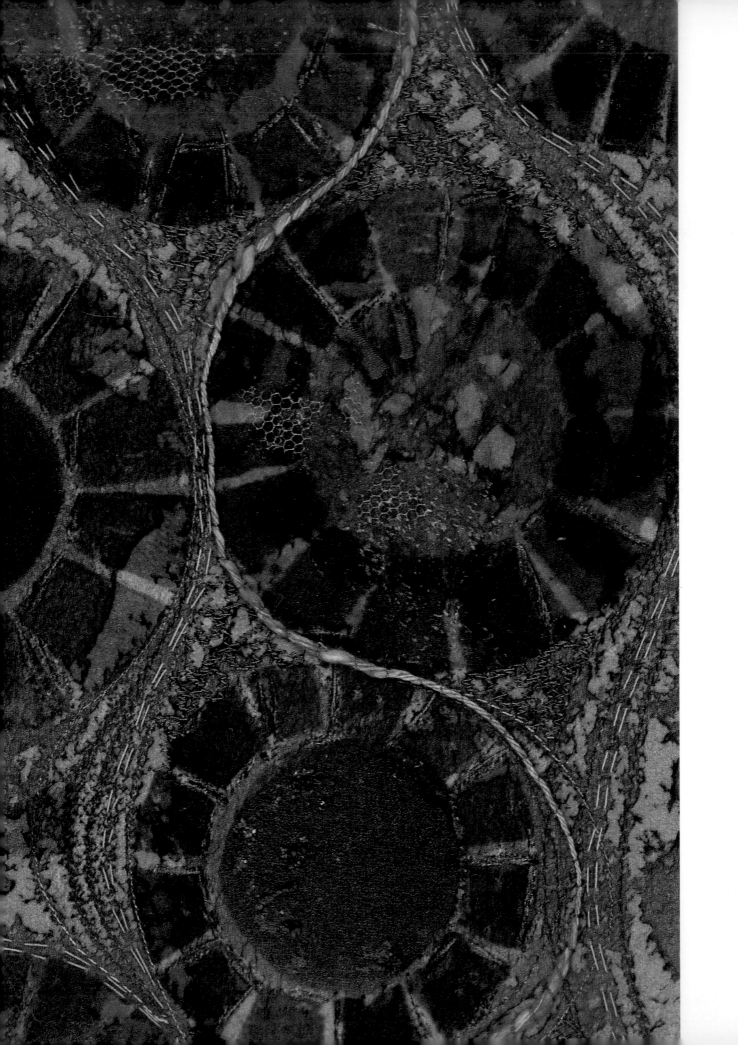

hot *textiles*

Inspiration and techniques with heat tools

Kim Thittichai

BATSFORD

Acknowledgments

This book is dedicated to Maeve Edwards, an inspirational tutor.

I would like to thank my lovely students of the past seven years. We made a wonderful journey together. As we have all discovered, you are never too old to learn, and the more you learn, the more you realize there is to learn.

I am forever indebted to my friends and family, who have stood by me and supported me all the way through my rather circuitous route to this exciting point.

Special thanks to Mary Sleigh.

First published in the United Kingdom in 2007 by
Batsford
10 Southcombe Street
London W14 0RA

An imprint of Anova Books Company Ltd

ISBN-13 9780713490404

A CIP catalogue record for this book is available from the British Library.

15 14 13 12 11 10 09 08
10 9 8 7 6 5 4 3 2

Reproduction by Spectrum Colour Ltd, England
Printed by Craft Print International Ltd, Singapore

This book can be ordered direct from the publisher at the website: www.anovabooks.com, or try your local bookshop.

Distributed in the United States and Canada by Sterling Publishing Co., 387 Park Avenue South, New York, NY 10016, USA.

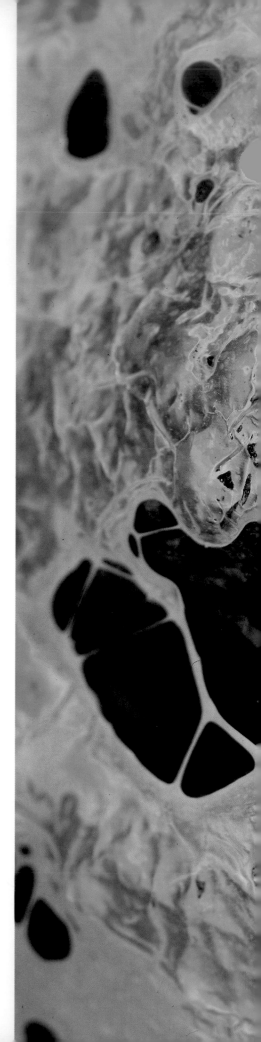

Front cover: Detail of work by Sue Davies (see page 25).

Page 2: Detail of work by Jan Eldridge (see page 118).

Right: Detail of bowl by Sarah Hawkins (see page 103).

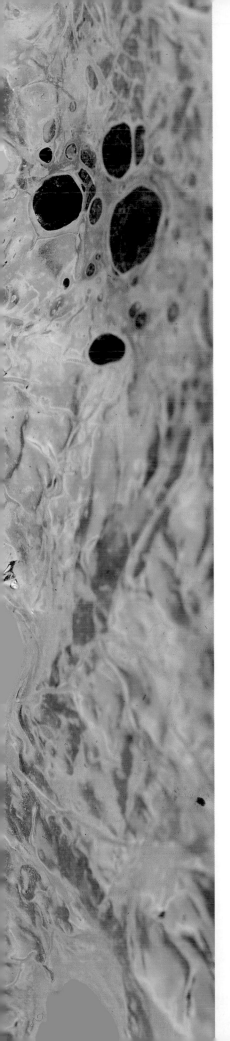

Contents

Introduction

Welcome to *Hot Textiles*. Whether this is your first foray into the exciting world of using heat to work textiles, or whether you already have some experience, there is always something new to learn.

My early training at Brighton Polytechnic (now Brighton University), UK, was in three-dimensional design of wood, metal, ceramics and plastics – I specialized in ceramics and silver. It was not until 1985, as part of my Creative Embroidery diploma at Brighton, that I started paying serious attention to using melted materials (initially plastic bags) in my embroidery work. Both these courses encouraged experimentation with materials before starting to design a piece of work. 'Learning through play' isn't just for toddlers; for an artist it is a very important part of developing your skills and exploring techniques.

Since then I have developed various processes involving plastic bags, cellophane, Bondaweb (Wonder-Under) and Tyvek. Layering materials and techniques has become a favourite way of creating amazing surfaces to stitch.

I came to teaching experimental textiles by a rather circuitous route in 1996. I originally taught traditional courses, but after a while I started to get bored. With my rather mixed training, I find it difficult to keep to traditional courses, and my instincts are to wander away from the narrow path and find out 'what happens if …'? While I fully appreciate the importance of learning traditional techniques, I have always been driven to push things further. I wrote and developed a new 30-week course, and 'Experimental Textiles' was born. After a slow start it took off, and has become a very successful course. The techniques I have chosen for this book are the ones I have found the most fun and most useful in my teaching, but there are many more.

Functional versus non-functional

My work is constantly changing as I learn and develop new methods with new materials. I am basically a three-dimensional textile artist. Because most of my work is non-functional – neither clothing nor lighting fixtures nor any other 'useful' object – I am continually asked, 'but what's it for?' Most of my large vessels are just that – large vessels. They just stand there, hopefully looking beautiful. I have tried putting lights in them to make them functional, but I feel that I am compromising my work when I do.

I have no idea why I work the way I do; maybe it's my early training, or always wanting to be different. It certainly seems to be something I am driven to do – we all have to find our own path. My work gives me great pleasure and satisfaction, and I am very lucky to have worked with and learned from tutors whom I greatly respect.

Pelmet Vilene (Pellon) coloured with fabric paint then decorated with painted Bondaweb (Wonder-Under), sprinkled snipped threads, glitter, 3D Medium and hand stitch.

I hope this book will both educate and inspire you. The most important thing to remember when trying any of the techniques in this book is to have fun, but safely.

I know it is annoying to have to stop and think before you create but I can't stress enough how important safety is when working with hot tools. If you can get into a safe routine every time you pick up your iron or heat gun you will be the healthier for it.

I hope this book will also excite you. I have included work – ranging from craft right through to fine art – of various students and textile artists, whose contact details are at the back of the book. It is a great privilege to be able to include work that I admire.

Part 1
Tools and Techniques

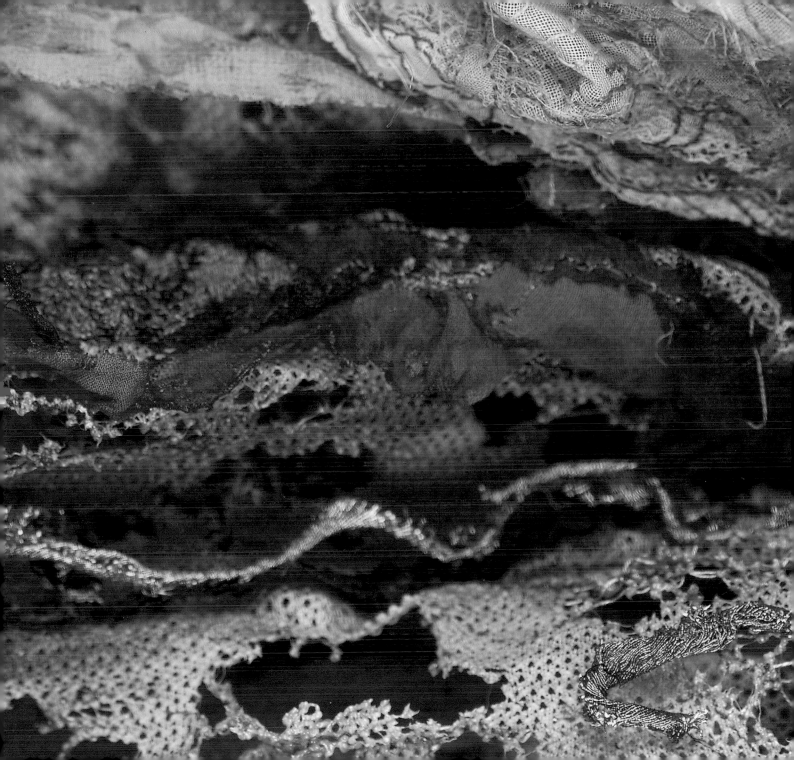

Before You Start...

Few of us are lucky enough to have a dedicated work space with specialist tools and equipment; we all muddle along, cutting corners where we judge it expedient. As far as I am aware from my experience, and from interviewing manufacturers and suppliers of products used in this book, none of the materials are life-threatening except perhaps plastic bags. They can be dangerous when melted in large amounts, say 50 at a time. Even melting that amount won't kill you, but you could give yourself a really bad headache. If you have any kind of breathing problem or are pregnant take great care and if in doubt, don't!

Whatever you are doing, even if it is just sitting quietly stitching, a well-ventilated room will help keep you alert and feeling better. If you are unsure of the properties of the product you are melting, work outside the house in the garden, or failing that, open all the windows. I have never suffered any ill effects from the processes covered in this book, but we are all different and the components of materials are changing all the time.

Be aware of the safety of any children and animals around you, in particular when using heat tools and dyes.

- Separate fabrics into natural and synthetic fibres.
- Work on a stable, protected surface.
- Check the flexes on your tools. They should be straight and free of kinks so that no one trips over them.
- Have a roll of baking parchment/paper to hand.
- Make sure you are working in a well-ventilated area.
- Keep a notebook of successes and failures.

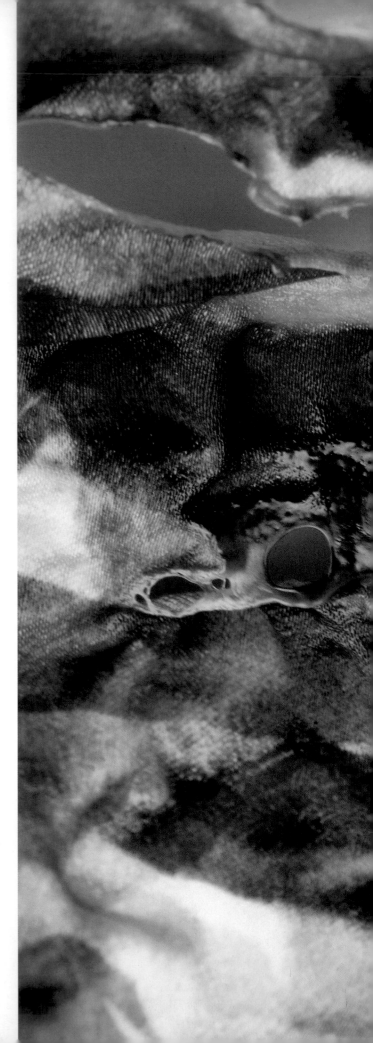

White acetate satin that has been transfer printed with disperse dyes then distressed with a heat gun.

Synthetic and natural

You can check if your fabric is synthetic by applying a heat gun to a corner of it (see Tools, page 14). Synthetic fabrics melt while natural fabrics burn, so if it puckers it is synthetic, if it starts to turn brown it is natural, or a mix with a certain amount of natural fibre in it. If your fabric starts to turn brown – STOP. It means your fabric is on the way to catching fire.

Your work surface

Don't be tempted to use the iron and ironing board you use to iron your clothes; they will get contaminated very quickly no matter how careful you are. Irons can be bought very cheaply from your local supermarket. You do not need a steam iron for any of the techniques in this book.

Working on a towel or old curtain covered with baking parchment/paper on a stable table is quite sufficient, and means you can set up anywhere.

Materials

Keep your range of materials small; don't expect to try everything at once. It is better to work through individual materials first, discovering their potential and limits. Once you are confident you know what a single material can do, you can then start to layer different materials. It would be a shame to miss something for the sake of another hour of experimentation.

Plastic shopping bags and bin liners shouldn't give off fumes when melted, especially in the small volumes that we use. But – and it is a big but – manufacturing processes are constantly changing, and one can never be sure what compounds might be included in the plastic one is using. If you are working in a well-ventilated space there should be no problem, but if you start to get a headache – STOP!

If you start to create a piece of work and you are apprehensive about choosing colours, stick to harmonious tones. If you are working with complex or varied textures, on the other hand, you don't need a lot of colour variation as well. The brain can only cope with so much information.

Learning through play

How can you design something if you don't know what the materials you are using will do, and how the techniques work? While it is important to be able to design a piece of work, greater importance needs to be placed on learning through play. If you are relaxed and enjoying your experiments you will remember much more, and this will be helped further by making notes. Inspiration can strike at the strangest times, so try to carry a small notebook and pen with you at all times to jot down ideas or sketches.

Stress can be a barrier to creativity. If you feel 'blank', just 'play' with your materials and don't pressurize yourself. You may be pleasantly surprised at the ideas that start to form.

It is wonderful to have a pallet of techniques to work from, but be warned: don't throw everything you know at one piece of work or it will look like a dog's breakfast. Build up slowly. Jae Maries's 1999 article 'The Butterfly Approach to Embroidery' warned of the dangers of being a 'technique junkie':

> *'This, in my opinion, is textile art's major drawback. There are so many techniques to try that you can easily become wooed by the technique itself rather than asking yourself if this method of working is really appropriate for your subject matter. The individuality of the creative embroiderer becomes obscured by technique and that personal voice that will distinguish your work from your neighbour's in an exhibition will be smothered by the technique itself.*
>
> *All of us need time to master and develop a technique for our own use and make it work for us. It should become a tool to help us externalise our ideas and say something personal. We may dabble forever and never get focused, like the butterfly fluttering from one seductive flower to another.'*

Heat-gunned polyester organza.

'The Butterfly Approach to Embroidery', Jae Maries, *The World of Embroidery* magazine, July 1999, Vol 50, no 4 page 219.

a

b

Tools

There are many tools available for craft and textiles, but the following are the ones I use most regularly and are featured in this book.

Heat gun

Heat guns or hot-air tools (a) have been used for heat embossing on cards and for scrapbooking for several years now. They are slowly coming into the domain of textiles. There are two basic wattages, 300 and 350. The 300-watt gun is most suitable for melting embossing powders, plastic bags and 'Tyvek'. The 350-watt gun can melt synthetic fabrics as well. Bead-making is much faster with a 350-watt gun.

Iron

Irons (b) come in many shapes and sizes. The wattage can vary considerably from one manufacturer to another. A basic model from your local supermarket will be perfectly adequate. It is not necessary to use steam for any of the techniques in this book.

'Clover' iron

The 'clover' iron (c) is a very small iron on a handle; it can be very useful for getting into awkward places that a normal iron can't reach, and can also be used on its side for foiling.

c   d   e

Soldering iron, Fabric Master and Gem Master

The soldering iron (d) is a wonderful tool for making marks and fusing fabrics together. There are various soldering irons to choose from; textile people tend to use the range between 18 and 20 watts. Don't be tempted to buy a cheap one from your local car parts store. Those models will be at least 30 watts, and will probably melt through the table you are working on as well as your work.

There are soldering irons with single fine ends and others with a selection of ends, such as the Fabric Master (e). There are tools with different brands for pyrography (the craft of burning designs into wood, leather or other materials), such as the Pyromaster, which can be used to great effect on textile projects.

The Gem Master (f) sets self-adhesive gemstones onto virtually any surface, which is great fun for that extra sparkle. Remember always to use a stand to support your soldering iron when you are working.

Respirator

A respirator (g) is a type of mask you need when there is a possibility of creating toxic fumes. These can be bought from your local hardware store. Note that these are *not* the more simple white particle masks – which you *should* wear when using fine powders such as dyes and powdered metals. A respirator creates a firm seal around the mouth and nose, and has filters that can be changed. You will look like Darth Vader and frighten the children – but you shouldn't take chances with your health.

g

f

Materials

From left to right: Plastic
shopping bags, Cello-Foil,
polyester organza and
fusible film.

These are the materials I use most regularly and are featured throughout this book, though there are many others available for craft and textiles.

Tyvek

Tyvek is 100 per cent spun polyester, and won't give off fumes when heated. There are several different weights. I only mention two in this book.
Heavyweight – stiff and paper-like. Heavy enough to go through an inkjet printer.
Lightweight – soft, fabric-like texture.
All weights can be moulded when hot, can be layered, and make fantastic beads.

Pelmet Vilene (Pellon)

Pelmet Vilene (Pellon) is a heavy, sew-in interfacing that takes dye and transfer paint well. It is a suitable weight for small boxes, soft book covers and small vessels. It is heavy enough to be machine-stitched without a frame, and is sold by the metre.

Heavy Pelmet Vilene Plus

This is a new interfacing, much stiffer than the Pelmet Vilene, and has the added advantage of a layer of fusible web on one side. The fusible side can be painted, foiled or decorated in the same way as Bondaweb (Wonder-Under). It can be carved with a soldering iron and takes colour in the same way as Pelmet Vilene. Because of its strength this product is excellent for making boxes and large three-dimensional vessels, and is sold by the metre.

Cello-Foil

This product is a cross between cellophane and foil, and has similar properties to cellophane. Its appearance is very metallic and shiny, with a choice of colours on one side and silver on the other. It responds to heat very quickly.

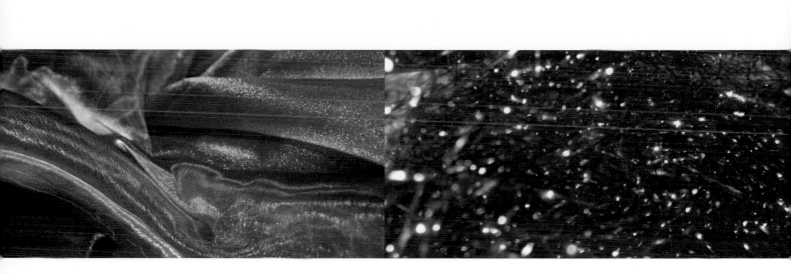

Lutradur

Lutradur is a non-woven polyester fabric that is great for three-dimensional work. It is intended for industrial use, with a wide variety of weights for different purposes, from the purely decorative (florists use it as wrapping) to the seriously heavyweight (agriculture and road building), and is sold by the metre. You can dye it, paint it, cut it up (it doesn't fray), use it by itself or, because of the translucent nature of the construction of the cloth, use the lightweight type on top of other patterned cloth without the handling problems of voiles and other lightweight fabrics. This exciting product can be treated and coloured in the same way as Pelmet Vilene, but can then be heat-gunned to create amazing textures.

Fusible film and fibres

A thin synthetic iridescent film that comes in a range of colours and can be ironed and heat-gunned to great effect. It makes great beads. The fibres have been around for two or three years but this very versatile film is a new addition.

Plastic shopping bags

Plastic shopping bags, bin liners, and clear plastic bags should be ironed between baking parchment. Most plastics will stick together, though after combining two or three layers they will become quite stiff after cooling down. They are most effective when used to make beads, and for moulding into bowls. For safety's sake, always ensure that you are wearing gloves (not rubber ones!) when handling hot melting plastic. I generally wear suede gardening gloves.

Polyester organza

This fabric, which is sold by the metre, can be heat-gunned and soldered to great effect. It is very useful as an overlay and makes splendid beads.

Cellophane

The type of sturdy cellophane used to wrap flowers, whether clear or patterned, can be ironed between baking parchment, though unlike plastic bags, it won't stick to itself. Like plastic bags, however, it is great for beads and for moulding into bowls.

Lazertran silk

This is an image-transfer paper made by Lazertran, which can be used with a toner-based laser printer or photocopier. It has been specifically developed for use with silk and satin. When your image had been transferred it can be foiled.

Bondaweb (Wonder-Under)

This fusible web, sold by the metre and in packs, can be painted and ironed onto fabric and paper. The resulting web of glue can then be decorated with threads, foils, leaves and so on.

Baking parchment

This silicone-treated, non-stick paper is a vital part of your equipment list. All the processes using an iron detailed in this book require it. You can't use your iron without it! It is sold by the roll and can be found in your local supermarket.

3D Medium or Xpandaprint

This is a paste that can be painted or stamped onto your work and expanded with a heat gun. The expanded paste creates a soft rubbery texture that can be stitched into and painted. Be warned – a little goes a long way.

Synthetic fabrics

You can experiment with fabrics such as acetate, acrylic, nylon or polyester to see how they respond to the heat gun. Synthetic fabrics make great beads and can be transfer printed.

A selection of
water-based paints.

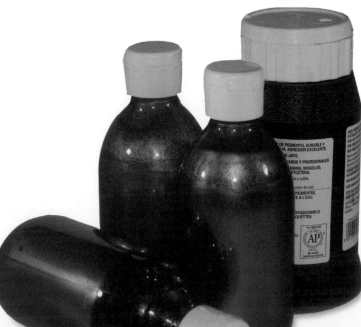

Heat-transfer foils

These foils can be used cold with foil glue and double-sided tape or, as I use them in this book, with an iron and Bondaweb (Wonder-Under). Heat-transfer foils are always used colour-side up; the foil is on the underside of a plastic carrier sheet.

Kunin felt

This felt is 100 per cent acrylic and can be heat-gunned to create amazing lacy textures. I use only grey, black or white from Winnifred Cottage (see suppliers list, page 126), as they are guaranteed not to be flame-guarded. Kunin felt can be dyed and printed with transfer paint. Its ability to be moulded when hot makes it great for creating beads; it can also be easily cut with a soldering iron.

Lamifix

This is a clear plastic film that can be ironed onto your work to seal it. It is washable up to 40°C (104°F), and is sold by the metre.

Paints

Oil-based paints will give off fumes when heated, so should be avoided for this kind of work. All the paints used in the projects detailed in this book are water based – I generally use acrylic or poster paints. None of the processes described here are washable, so cheap paints will work as well as more expensive ones.

Vanishing muslin and Thermogauze

Vanishing muslin is a chemically treated cotton that can be dissolved with a heat gun or iron, or by being placed on a baking sheet in a preheated moderate oven for 5 minutes. Thermogauze is a heavyweight muslin that can be transfer-printed with a warm iron, then parts can be zapped away with a heat gun.

Acrylic wax

Acrylic wax is my favourite way of sealing work. It is less shiny than varnish. The wax dries to a waterproof finish and the brushes used to apply it can be washed out in water.

A selection of
heat-transfer foils.

Bark cloth

The soft inner bark of certain trees from the tropics can be effective in textile work. The pieces I used are generally tan in colour, with an interesting texture. No two pieces are the same.

Hot-fix rhinestones and gems

The gems and crystals have glue on the back and can be applied with an iron or Gem Master to almost anything you wish in the textile and craft field.

Embossing powders

Embossing powders are dry granules of heat-responsive resin that melt at 100–120°C (212–248°F). They are best heated with a heat gun. They give a wonderful shine and need to be applied with some kind of glue or ink to stop them from blowing away.

Water-soluble paper

This paper is quite magical to work with. It works well as a support for free machine embroidery and 3D Medium. There are many other uses. Experiment!

Procion dyes

I use Procion dyes to dye all natural fabrics apart from wool (wool needs a different type of dye). Procion dyes also work well when painted onto Pelmet Vilene (Pellon) and Heavy Pelmet Vilene Plus.

The fusible web side of the Heavy Pelmet Vilene Plus retains its adhesive properties when painted with dye. Procion dyes can be thickened if you wish to print with them. Always refer to the manufacturer's instructions.

Disperse dyes

Disperse dyes colour synthetic fabrics. They can be transfer-printed onto fabric or used as a hot-water dye. Disperse dyes produce wonderful bright, clear and transparent colour. Disperse dyes can be thickened if you wish to print with them. Always refer to the manufacturer's instructions.

Magic film

This heat-soluble plastic film has been created to assist when machine embroidering on towelling and velvet but has another use. The film can be painted with acrylic paint and then heat-gunned to create wonderful surfaces. You can also try transfer printing on magic film, but use a low heat.

The Iron

Always iron on a flat, stable surface. If you use an ironing board, I recommend having a dedicated ironing board cover and iron for your textile work – irons can be bought very cheaply these days. A tiny, stray piece of Bondaweb (Wonder-Under) in the wrong place can cause havoc with your iron and the pile of clothes you were planning to iron!

For textile work I tend to use a table covered with an old towel and three layers of baking parchment. A steam iron is not necessary for any of the materials or techniques described in this book.

An iron is extremely versatile; it can be used to apply Bondaweb (Wonder-Under), hot-fix gems, heat-transfer foils, image-transfer papers and transfer paints or disperse dyes. You can also use an iron to melt plastic bags, cellophane, chocolate wrappers and Tyvek – use sheets of baking parchment between layers to protect the iron.

Chocolate wrappers (above) and plastic bags (below), fused together by ironing them between baking parchment.

Sort out all the interesting pieces of plastic and sweet papers you have been hoarding. Try layering several pieces of variously coloured plastic bags onto a sheet of baking parchment; lay another sheet of baking parchment on top and iron slowly and continuously with a hot iron for approximately one minute. The plastic will melt and stick to itself. While the piece is hot you can stretch and shape it. Remember *always* to wear gloves – such as suede gardening gloves – if you are handling hot plastic.

Photocopied paper or card can be foiled. Old-fashioned black-and-white photocopiers use the correct toner. Photocopy your design onto paper or light card and iron foil onto it. The foil will stick to the toner. This is a great technique for card making.

Lazertran silk can also be used in conjunction with photocopying, to transfer a design onto silk or satin, which can then be foiled. The paper is fed through a laser printer or a photocopier in black-and-white mode, is ironed onto your chosen fabric, soaked in water, the backing paper removed and then ironed dry. The black transferred image can then be foiled. Always use two sheets of baking parchment, one to protect your work surface, and one to protect your iron and fabric. The Lazertran company have various papers, which between them can transfer your image onto just about any surface.

This image has been transferred onto silk then foiled.

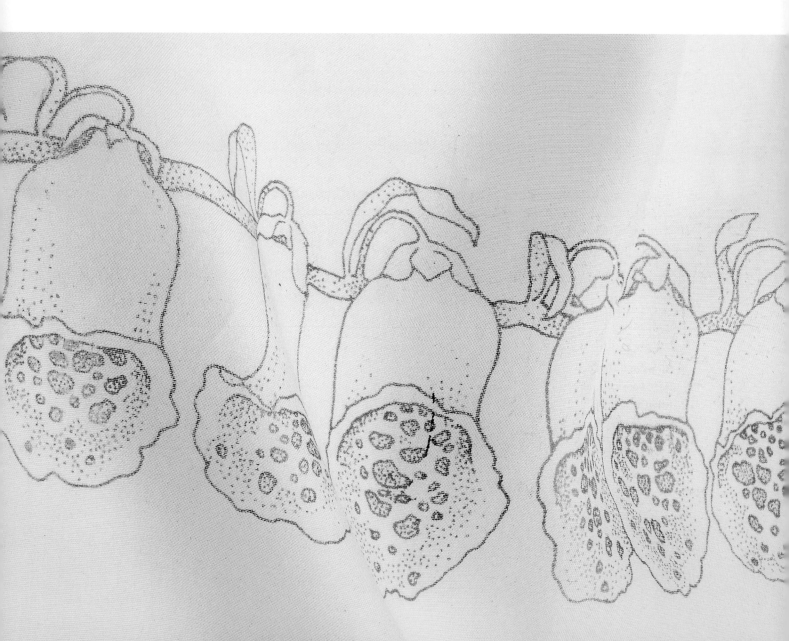

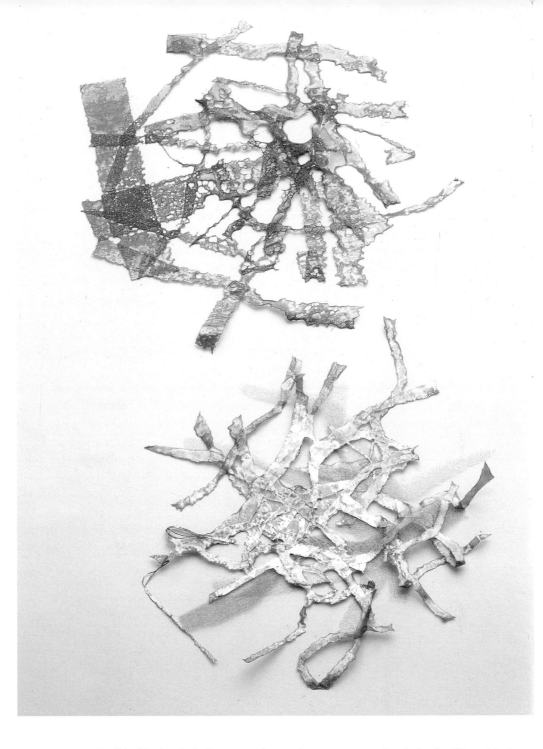

Strips of fusible film that
have been fused together
using an iron.

Fusible film is relatively new to the market – you may already be familiar with the stranded variety. The film can be cut, stamped, heated with a heat gun and fused together with an iron. Try cutting six or seven randomly sized strips, placing them between baking parchment and ironing them quickly with a medium heat iron. The film will fuse together. Try incorporating the film with plastic bags so that the two materials stick together. Or intermingle fine strips of polyester organza and fusible film. The fabric won't stick to the film, but if you sandwich it all together it should all meld.

The iron is invaluable for transfer printing. This process is covered on page 46.

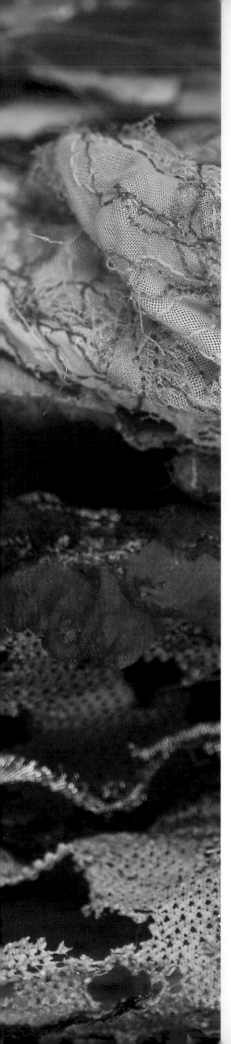

Heat Guns

I don't want to spoil your fun before you start, but it is very important to note one or two health and safety rules regarding heat guns.

ALWAYS work in a well-ventilated room. Fumes can build up, even from apparently innocuous materials, without you realizing it. We all get carried away at times and put off getting up to open a window until we've finished the bit we're doing. Half an hour later you could have a very bad headache, or worse, that could have been avoided. If you are pregnant, or have any kind of breathing difficulties such as asthma, I would recommend you wear a proper respirator. Never heat polystyrene.

Work on a stable surface, preferably a table where you can spread out all the materials you are working with and find them quickly and safely. A towel laid on the table, covered with a piece of baking parchment, makes an excellent 'ironing board'.

There are various brands of heat guns with various wattages. My favourite is a 350-watt gun. This is hot enough to melt thick synthetic fabrics quite fast and does wonders with laminated layers of plastic bags.

When you are working with a heat gun the nozzle needs to be a minimum of 25mm (1in) from your work. If you get any closer the air can't circulate around the gun and the internal thermostat will cause it to cut out to prevent overheating. For this reason, if you have been working continuously for half an hour you may find your gun just stops working. Work on something else for about thirty minutes, and it will start again.

The correct distance to hold your heat gun away from your work is approximately 2.5cm (1in).

These wonderful decaying pods by Sue Davies are made from various synthetic fabrics and threads that have been distressed with a heat gun.

Paint-stripping guns are tempting to use, but be careful – they can be very powerful. The nozzle is wider and will therefore blow your work around more. Two-speed models are more controllable.

Heat guns, easily available by mail order, are a better, more controllable tool for textiles as they have a stand, which means they can be used 'hands free'. This is particularly useful when making beads. When using your heat gun don't be tempted to 'waggle' it about. Hold the gun at right angles to your work and aim it at your work steadily and precisely, keeping it focused on one place till the work starts to bubble before moving it around. Unless you are working with thin polyester organza, 'waggling' will not make the work sufficiently hot. To make it pliable, or to melt it, you need to let the heat build up.

Making beads

To make fantastic beads, all you need is:

- A heat gun.
- A metal knitting needle (not a plastic one).
- Synthetic fabric, fusible film, Kunin felt, cellophane or plastic bags.
- Fine wire to stop your bead unravelling.

Wrap strips of your chosen material around the knitting needle. If you want extra texture, try twisting your material as you wrap. Hold the strips in place by wrapping a short length of wire around them, and heat them, holding your heat gun a minimum of 25mm (1in) from the material until it begins to melt and bubble.

Remember that the metal needle will get hot at the end you are heating, so take care not to burn the hand you are holding it with. I have tried using a wooden satay stick soaked in water and wrapped in baking parchment to protect my fingers from heat travelling down the stick, but I find it all a bit fiddly. Just be careful and try to use the longest knitting needle you can find – but always make sure it's not a plastic one, or it will melt! Wear a glove on the hand holding the needle as it can get hot. If you feel you need both hands free to manipulate the materials put your heat gun onto its stand.

When cooled and hardened, the round strips of material around the shaft of the needle will have formed beads. Wait for them to cool before you take the wire off. Occasionally the wire will melt into the bead, but you can leave this as a decorative effect.

A collection of beads
made from various
synthetic fabrics.

Work with single materials to start with to get a feel
for what works well. You could try:

- Painted Tyvek
- Plastic bags
- Cellophane
- Fusible film
- Plastic fruit nets (the type oranges come in)
- Sweet or chocolate wrappers
- Kunin felt
- Polyester organza
- Synthetic fabrics, polyester, acetate, nylon
  and so on.

If you want to use your beads to make a necklace, but
they feel rough and spiky, just roll them on your work
table while they are still hot to smooth them off.
Make sure you protect your hands from the hot
material at all times.

Once you feel confident, try mixing your materials,
making a variety of sizes. Here are a few ideas:

- Plastic bags wrapped with sequin waste
- Several different colours of polyester organza
- Tyvek and polyester organza
- Synthetic fabric
- Cellophane and plastic

A selection of beads made from polyester organza.

When you have made a varied selection of beads, try decorating them. I am sure you can think of many embellishments, but here are a few to get you started:

- Embroidery threads and fine, textured knitting yarns
- Small glass beads threaded on to fine wire
- Glitter glue

There are several ways of using your beads. I use them to make bowls and vessels. To do this I thread the beads onto a firm wire and then coil them into a bowl shape (if you ever made coil pots in school art class, it is a similar process). The wire is then stitched together to hold it in shape. Here are some further uses for beads:

Necklaces
Thread a selection of beads onto beading wire. Try interspersing your beads with metal or glass ones. The contrast of smooth and spiky textures can be quite beautiful.

Brooches
Large, decorated beads can be made into brooches by threading them onto a large safety or nappy pin.

Tassels
Beads make wonderfully mad tassels. Just thread the tails of your tassels through a large bead and anchor with a braid or thick knitting yarn.

Bag handles
There is a big trend for felted bags at the moment. Plastic beads threaded onto firm fencing wire make unusual and strong bag handles. Melted beads can also be stitched on to decorate the bags. The beads create an interesting contrast of textures.

Buttons
Try using plastic bag beads as buttons on heavy knitted cardigans and jackets. Plastic beads will be very strong and will withstand hand washing.

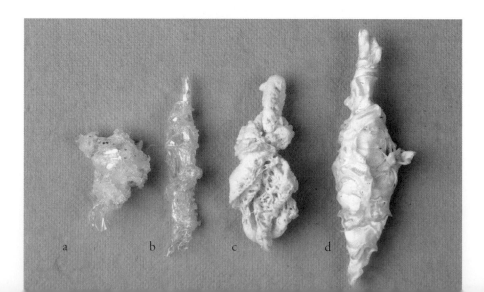

Beads made from cellophane (a and b), Kunin felt (c) and acetate satin (d).

This little bowl was
constructed from beads
made from sweet
wrappers. The beads were
threaded onto firm wirc
then coiled into shape and
stitched to hold the bowl
together.

Beads made from plastic
shopping bags (see detail,
left) were threaded onto
wire then coiled and stitched
to form a bowl (below).

Other uses for your heat gun

When using an iron to heat plastics and cellophane you end up with a reasonably flat piece of work. But a heat gun can create a three-dimensional shape. There is nothing to restrict your work and it will bubble and twist freely. Try heat-gunning different shapes and thicknesses of fabric. You will need to hold your fabric or plastic down so that the air expelled from the heat gun doesn't blow the work all over the table. Whatever you use to pin it down needs to be at least 30cm (12in) long. I use whatever is lurking on my work table, such as a metal knitting needle or a long pair of dressmaking scissors. The crucial point is not to use your fingers to hold down your work, as you will burn them.

Fusible film can be fused and melted together with an iron. But once you have ironed the film try heat-gunning it. For crazy, twisted effects just cut your film into shapes and heat-gun them. Try this with pieces of plastic bag of approximately A4 size – 210 x 297mm (8¼ x 11¾in) – and see what happens.

Strips of fusible film have been fused together with an iron then heat-gunned for extra texture.

3D Medium or Xpandaprint

This sample by Sally Colledge is a section of a much larger hanging entitled *Urchin*. The piece hangs from the ceiling and is 3m (10ft) long. It is based on tentacles. Five 3m- (10ft-) long, 75mm- (3in-) wide strips of polyester organza were painstakingly painted with small regular dots of 3D Medium. The 3D Medium was then expanded with a heat gun to create a wonderful sucker-like effect.

3D Medium or Xpandaprint is a cream paste that is applied sparingly and heat gunned to create an amazing bubbly texture that can be painted with acrylic paints once it has cooled down. Please be warned: a little goes a long way. The paste can be printed onto a surface with printing blocks or painted on with a brush. It is then heat-gunned, and expands dramatically.

Detail of *Urchin* by Sally Colledge. 3D Medium applied to polyester organza then expanded with a heat gun.

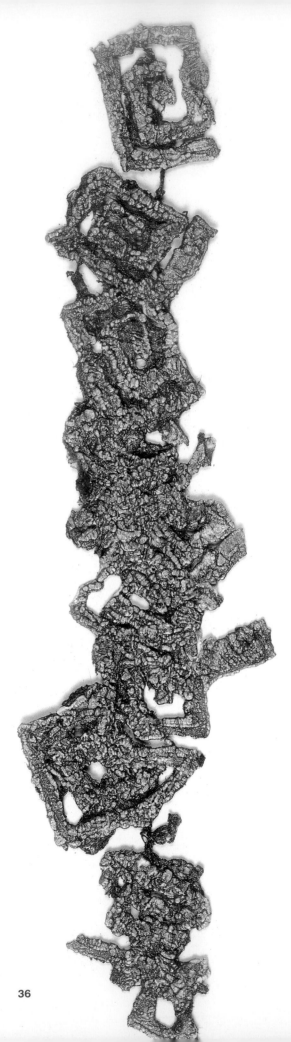

3D Medium can also be used to great effect on water-soluble paper. To create this edge for a vessel I took a machine stitch for a walk, creating a chain of stitch that linked together. This is the most important part of the process, because if the stitches are not joined together your work will fall apart. I then applied the 3D Medium with a rubber stamp over the machine stitch. The 3D Medium was then heat-gunned to expand it (please note that you will lose the sharp edge of a stamped image as the 3D Medium expands). The 3D Medium was then painted with a waterproof paint – acrylic or glass paints are quite suitable. (If the paint isn't waterproof your beautiful piece of work will wash away down the sink.) Once the paint was dry I carefully washed away the paper. The beautiful textured surface can be added to the edge of a bowl, down the side of a book cover, or applied in a number of other ways.

Stamped and expanded 3D Medium has been used to create an edge for the rim of a small vessel.

Layers

The heat gun can help to create wonderful layered pieces. Try combining alternate layers of heavyweight Tyvek with polyester organza, stitched together by hand or machine with natural thread (synthetic threads will melt). Then heat-gun gently, building up the heat slowly, working on both sides so the work doesn't curl up in just one direction. Once you have distressed your work, try applying foil to the surface with the iron.

Kunin felt is one of my favourite fabrics to work with. It has not been flame-guarded during manufacture, so will distress when heated with a heat gun. It can also be dyed, or transfer-printed with disperse dyes. Try applying painted Bondaweb (Wonder-Under) to Kunin felt and then foiling the Bondaweb (Wonder-Under). Heat-gun the whole piece to create a beautiful, lacy texture. To create wonderful edges, run your heat gun down the length of the Kunin felt in a line until the felt is lacy, then wait for it to cool and pull it gently apart. Try decorating the work with Kunin beads.

A 29.5 x 21cm (11¾ x 8¼in) piece of black kunin felt, decorated with painted Bondaweb (Wonder-Under) and heat gunned to create lacy-edged strips. The strips were then applied to orange cotton velvet and a final layer of embossing powder added.

Lutradur is a relatively new product to the textile market. It is made from spun polyester and comes in various weights. It will take dyes, paint and transfer paints. The sample shown below has been dyed with Procion dye and then heat-gunned to show the beautiful texture that can be achieved. Lutradur has a very matt surface that would contrast well with very shiny materials.

A 29.5 x 21cm (11¾ x 8¼in) piece of heavy Lutradur, Procion-dyed and heat-gunned to create a wonderful, crusty effect.

Two layers of heavy Tyvek, layered with two layers of polyester organza. The whole thing was stitched together and then distressed with a heat gun.

Soldering Irons

Soldering irons are wonderfully versatile tools. They can be used to weld synthetic fabrics together and cut through synthetic fabrics, creating great sealed edges as they cut. They will also carve into heavy Pelmet Vilene (Pellon) and Vilene Plus. Margaret Beal has written a wonderful book about the welding technique, called *Fusing Fabric* (see further reading, page 127).

There are many different types of soldering iron on the market, including single fine-tipped ones, and ones with a choice of ends. Wattage can also vary, but around 18 watts is plenty for textile work. When using a soldering iron never apply too much pressure, particularly with the fine tips, as they can bend if used too vigorously. Just take your time, whether you are using your soldering iron to foil Bondaweb (Wonder-Under), carve Pelmet Vilene (Pellon) or bond sheer fabrics together. Since you are working with a fine point of heat, it takes time to do its job. Try these ideas:

- Use soldering irons to carve and make marks into Pelmet Vilene (Pellon) and Heavy Pelmet Vilene Plus.
- Use a soldering iron to cut your transfer-printed synthetic fabrics into strips and layer them up with toning prints.
- Bond synthetic fabrics together using a fine-tipped soldering iron: gently apply pressure where you wish the fabrics to bond. The marks that you make can become part of your design.
- Try making regular marks and building up patterns with your soldering iron.
- Make very organic wavy edges by using the soldering iron freehand, or create sharp edges by using a metal ruler.

This beautiful sample created by Margaret Beal has many layers of polyester organza that have been cut and shaped using a fine-tipped soldering iron.

Materials to experiment on with your soldering iron

Any fabric that is 100 per cent synthetic can be 'cut', or bonded together, with a soldering iron. Try the following:

- Plastic and polythene bags
- Polyester and nylon organza
- Acetate satin
- Kunin felt
- Foil food wrapping
- Cellophane
- Nylon chiffon scarves
- Transfer-printed plastic

It is always interesting to layer different materials together. Try combining two or three of the suggestions above. You could try heat-gunning your work if you feel it looks a bit flat.

Cream polyester, transfer printed with disperse dyes, was cut into strips with a fine-tipped soldering iron. The strips were then applied to another piece of similarly decorated polyester.

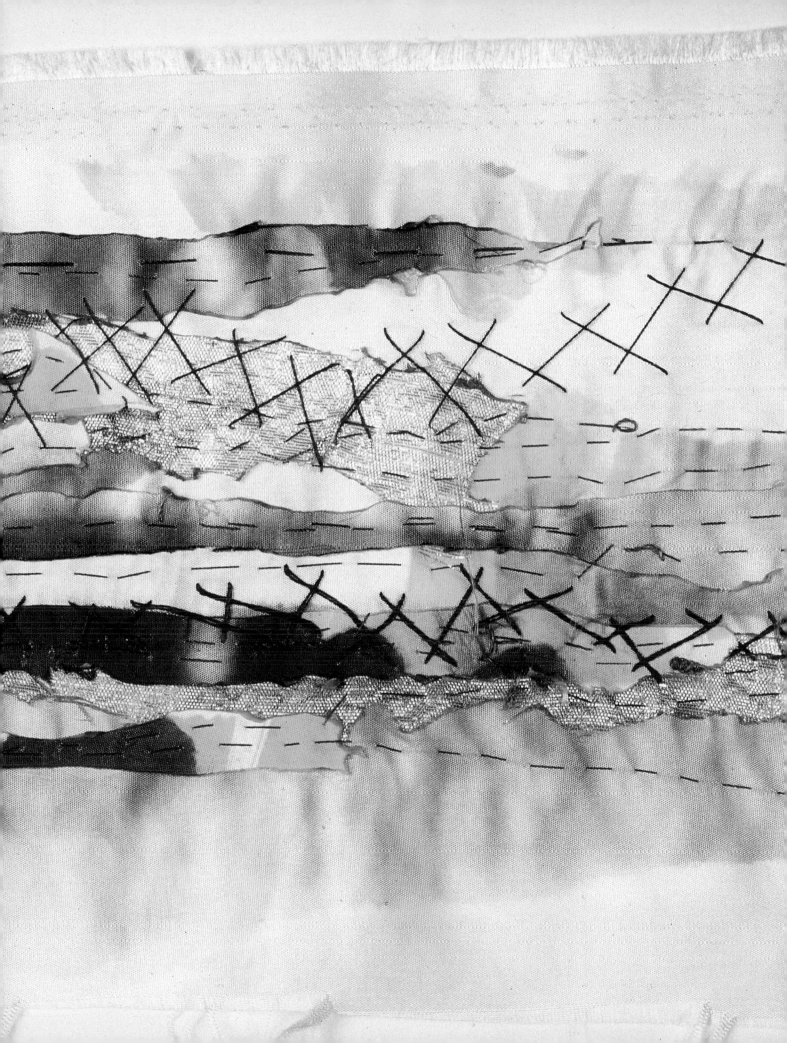

Using your soldering iron creatively

This sample (right) by Jan Eldridge has combined layers of polyester organza with a heavy black cotton background. The layers have been stitched together and a heat gun and soldering iron have been used to distress the top layers and expose the lower ones.

If you like a bit of sparkle on your work, then a soldering iron that applies hot-fix gems to any surface is great fun to use. These gems can be applied to clothing, hardback books and metal – whatever you fancy.

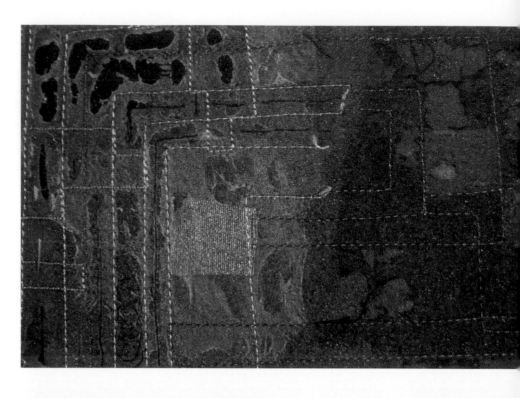

Sarah Sepe has created a stunning piece of work (right) using the soldering iron to pierce synthetic fabric. The work is inspired by pebbles on a beach. Synthetic suede has been layered and decorated by 'drawing' with a fine-tipped soldering iron. Threads have been added to give the piece texture.

These samples by Jan Eldridge (top) and Sarah Sepe (bottom) demonstrate how to use a soldering iron to create texture.

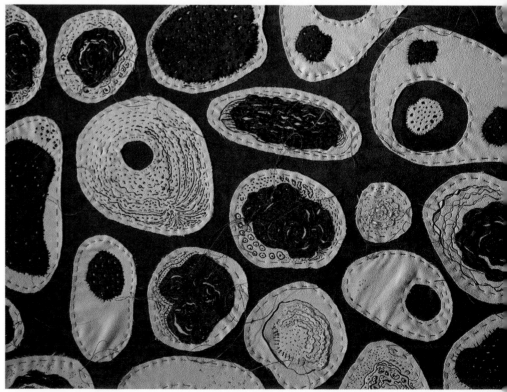

Colouring Synthetic Fabric

Working safely

- When using dye powders it is recommended that you wear a particle mask. Don't work in a draught where powders can drift on a breeze. Covering your work surface with damp newspaper will help stop any spilt powder from travelling any further, and will give you time to clean up spills.
- Always protect your hands with gloves, be they rubber or latex. Both are easily available form your supermarket or local hardware store. If you do get any dye on your skin, wash immediately with plenty of soap and water.
- When using dye, never use the same utensils and work surfaces that are used for food and drink preparation.
- If you have made up your powdered dye with water and have some left over, it can be stored in an air-tight container. Make sure you label the container and store away from any foodstuffs. The dye will have a shelf life of several years.
- Similarly any papers that have been painted with transfer dyes but that haven't been ironed off can be stored in a plastic sleeve (see page 46).
- Always use up small amounts of dye left in your mixing palette. Experiment with different ways of applying the dye – if you were going to throw it away anyway, you have nothing to lose.
- There is a certain amount of odour released when you heat disperse dyes, particularly when using the iron. Be sensible and open some windows. The dyes are non-toxic but fumes can still give you a headache!

Disperse dyes

Disperse dyes were developed in the early 1920s to dye the new synthetic fabrics that would not colour with established dyes. Using disperse dyes meant that these new fabrics could be dyed with colourfast colour without the use of water. Disperse dyes have been developed in powder and liquid forms, and are also available as crayons. There are many synthetic fabrics, from satin and chiffon to felt and velvet. Nylon, acetate and polyester, which all take disperse dyes extremely well, are the most well known (see Suppliers on page 26).

Work with a pale-coloured or white fabric for the brightest colour dyes. The dyes become fast when heated to 90–100°C (194–212°F). They can be applied to fabric in several ways; one of the most popular is transfer printing. Disperse dyes are transparent and will create amazing layered effects.

Transfer printing

The dye is painted or printed onto thin non-absorbent paper, such as photocopy paper. If the paper is absorbent, it will absorb the dye and you will have to work very hard to transfer the dye onto your fabric. Use the dyes as you would paint. They can be thinned to create more pastel shades, and can be thickened to print with.

The colours will look rather dull and uninspiring when you paint them onto your paper. But prepare to be amazed – they become vibrant when transferred to synthetic fabric. If you find the colours a little too bright, try transferring onto a natural fabric instead; this will make the colours more muted.

I find they work particularly well on Pelmet Vilene (Pellon), Lutradur and white or cream acetate or polyester satin. Following the manufacturer's instructions, the powdered dye is mixed with water and then painted onto smooth paper; photocopy paper is perfect for this. Once the paint is dry the design can be ironed off (painted-side down) onto your fabric of choice. Keep ironing your papers until there is no dye left (at least two or three times). Always use baking parchment to protect your ironing surface and between your iron and your work. These paints are permanent once they have been ironed off.

When you have successfully used transfer printing on fabric, try printing on clear polythene bags. Acetate sheets will also take a transfer print. Please bear in mind that the iron needs to be on a medium heat – there is a fine line between transferring your design and melting the plastic entirely. Thermogauze can also be transfer printed.

Resists or masks, which prevent the paint or dye reaching certain parts of the fabric, can be used between the transfer paper and fabric. Try using dry grasses and seeds or a paper doily. The most important thing to remember is to keep the iron moving. Transferring the design can take several minutes with a hot iron, and if you don't keep the iron moving

Transfer-printed
polyester satin.

you will have a print with the shape of the iron on it! Try not to move the paper as you iron – you will get a shadowed print. When working with fine fabrics such as polyester organza beware of melting the fabric. Turn the iron to the hottest temperature that your fabric can stand but no more; your fabric could melt to the paper. Although we are looking at melting and distressing in this book, melting is not part of this particular process.

Experiment with tearing your painted paper into strips, which will create beautiful shadowy effects. Lay the strips onto your fabric without overlapping them. Iron them off and then change the papers around. Do this three or four times until you have exhausted the painted papers (they get paler each time).

Transfer paints can be applied to the paper like any other paint, so try using rubber stamps and printing blocks. If you find the paint a bit thin when using your printing blocks you can add a thickener. Always remember that your designs will be reversed once it has been printed.

As you are printing onto synthetic fabric, once you have transferred your design, try heat-gunning your fabric and distressing your work.

Painting your papers

Always lay the paper you are painting on several protective layers of newspaper. If you are wanting special effects (some are listed below) the papers need to be well loaded with dye, and so will be quite wet. Depending on the heat and humidity in the room the papers can take up to 24 hours to dry. Bear this in mind if you have to leave papers out and there are children or animals around.

Different paint effects to try

- Once you have painted your disperse dye onto paper, sprinkle rock or sea salt crystals onto the wet surface and leave to dry. The crystals will draw in the dye and create a beautiful effect.
- Paint your paper with one or two colours, and while it is wet, place a sheet of crumpled clingfilm over the whole sheet of paper. This effect will take quite a time to dry. The clingfilm can be carefully peeled off once the paper is almost dry.
- Try 'ink blots'. Paint a small amount of dye in the middle of a piece of paper, fold the paper in half and press gently. The dye will splurge out into fabulous shapes. Try mixing two or three colours. Be careful not to apply too much dye, as this is likely to splurge out of the sides.
- When using two or three colours at a time allow them to bleed into each other.
- Using different tools to apply the dyes can create very individual effects. Rubber stamps are fun to use, but try something more basic. A sponge, a scrunched-up plastic bag, or bubblewrap all make fabulous backgrounds. The end of a piece of corrugated cardboard is one of my favourites.

Printing from paper bags

Transferring designs from printed paper bags is fun and free. They usually have a serrated edge and are dull in colour. You will get to know which ones transfer and which ones don't. The bags are made from the paper that is used to clean the rollers in the printing industry. Rather than throw the papers away, low-cost bags are made from them. Use the bags as pre-printed paper, and iron them with baking parchment the same way as if you had painted the paper yourself.

Using a photocopier

Photocopied designs can be painted with disperse dyes and transferred in the same way. The black toner from the photocopy will also transfer – but be warned: toner is not washable. This process is ideal if you are unsure of your drawing and painting skills. There are several books available containing copyright-free designs. Never use someone else's copyrighted design or photograph. Apart from being bad practice, it is unnecessary in these days of photocopiers and digital cameras. Even the most unsuccessful of your designs can be manipulated and reworked to your satisfaction.

Thermogauze

You can use transfer print on this heavyweight vanishing muslin and then distress it with a heat gun. Because the muslin is heat soluble the iron temperature should be low to medium. This means the print will not be very bright, but some print should transfer. Dissolve parts of the muslin with a heat gun to create a lovely worn look.

Magic film

This clear, heat-soluble film can be transfer printed with an iron on a medium heat. As always, remember to use baking parchment between the film and the iron. Allow the film to cool before removing the transfer painted paper. The film can then be heat-gunned to create wonderful textures. Try layering strips of the printed film with sheer fabrics for a beautifully 'light' effect.

Transfer crayons

Transfer crayons come in packets similar to wax crayons. There are several different brands. Transfer crayons are not to be confused with fabric crayons, which are applied by working directly onto the fabric and then ironed to fix. If in doubt, check the instructions on the back of the box: as long as they say to use the crayons on paper and then transfer them to fabric, they will be the correct ones.

Transfer crayons can be used either above or underneath disperse dyes. Try painting up your paper, letting it dry, and then adding a scribble or design in transfer crayon. Alternatively, draw onto your paper with a transfer crayon and then apply the disperse dye. The crayon will resist the dye.

The design on the paper bag (top) was transferred onto heavy Lutradur with an iron. This was then distressed with a heat gun (bottom).

Transfer crayons can also be melted before they are transferred, as follows:

1 Try grating and then spreading out a few colours onto your copy paper. Two teaspoons would be plenty.
2 Place baking parchment over the crayon and melt with the iron. Leave to cool right down.
3 When cool, remove the baking parchment.
4 Turn the decorated paper over and iron onto your fabric. The crayons will melt again and create either a wonderful design or a dreadful mess! Don't overdo the grated crayons; a little goes a long way. Keep to tones of one colour or at least restrict the number of colours that you use.
5 Try tearing up your papers or cutting out shapes before you iron them off.

Space dyeing in the microwave

There are few things more satisfying than working with fabrics that you have dyed yourself. As it is sometimes difficult to obtain Kunin felt that hasn't been flame-guarded. I have started to dye it myself. Being more confident generally about dyeing, I thought I would try working with disperse dyes in the microwave. I was very pleased with the result. I placed a 20cm- (8in-) square of wet white Kunin felt into a microwave-proof dish and, using a teaspoon, dribbled several colours of dye over the whole piece. As the felt is quite thick I massaged it (wearing strong rubber gloves) to encourage the dye to soak into the fabric. When I was happy with the amount of penetration, I covered the dish in clingfilm and mircowaved it on high power for three minutes. Please be aware that steam will build up, so be very careful when removing the clingfilm. Leave the dish to cool down. Wearing strong rubber gloves, rinse out your fabric until the water runs clear. The colours are more subdued compared to fabrics that have had the colour transferred by iron, but they do make wonderful background fabrics.

Another method is to sprinkle disperse dye powder directly onto wet fabric while it is in a microwave-proof dish and let it sit for a few minutes. The powders will bleed together and create beautiful effects. Cover with clingfilm, being careful not to disturb the effect. Microwave for three minutes on high. This method is particularly successful on white acetate satin. Be careful, when using dye powders, not to inhale them; you must also always wash your hands after using dyes.

Try dyeing nylon filament or fishing line. Put a length, loosely tied, into a plastic bag with your chosen dye and microwave on high for two minutes. Hot-water dyeing will also be effective for colouring this type of plastic (see opposite).

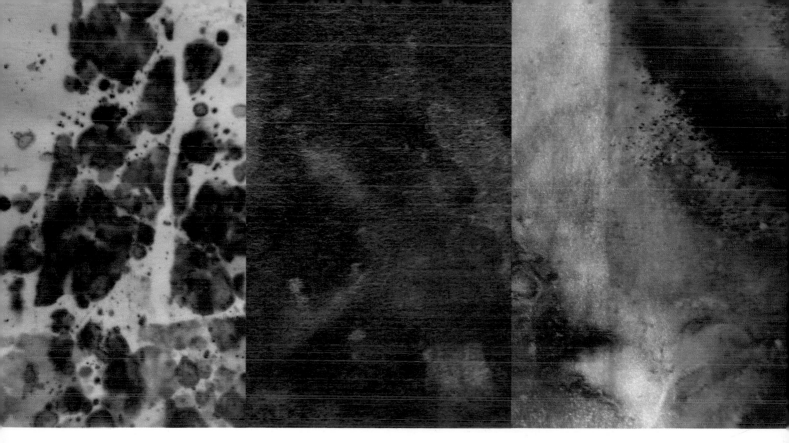

From left to right: grated and melted transfer crayons ironed onto white acetate satin; hot-water dyed Kunin felt; transfer dye powder sprinkled onto wet acetate satin and microwaved for three minutes (always wear a protective mask when sprinkling dye powders).

Hot-water dyeing

This process is good for creating a solid base colour, which can then be overprinted if you wish. Use a saucepan that you can dedicate to dyeing. Once you have used the pan to dye fabric you should no longer use it for food. A heavy-based pan is ideal. The pan needs to be large enough and deep enough to hold your fabric plus enough water to cover it.

Warm the water until it is hand-hot, then sprinkle a teaspoon of dye powder onto the water and stir with a metal spoon until the dye is dissolved. Add your damp synthetic fabric and heat it up slowly over 30 minutes to a slow simmer. Continue simmering for another 20 minutes. It is important to keep the fabric submerged and to keep stirring if you require an even colour. If you enjoy this process then try not disturbing the fabric and see what happens. It is possible to achieve a muted space-dyed effect.

Allow the fabric to cool and rinse until the waste water runs clear. Your fabric is now colourfast. Darker colours can be achieved by adding more dye, but bear in mind that if you want to print onto your fabric it will need to be reasonably pale. Let the fabric dry naturally and then iron it.

What next?
• Distress your fabric with a heat gun.
• Slash and cut your fabric with a soldering iron.
• Layer your fabric with transfer-printed Lutradur, stitch together and heat-gun through to expose different layers.

Whatever you do, have fun – safely!

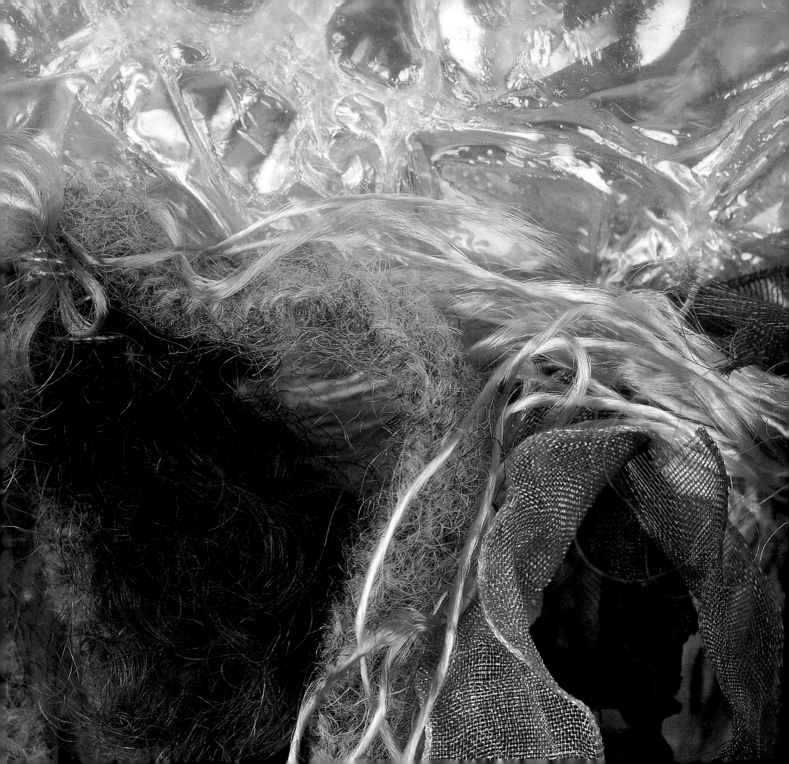

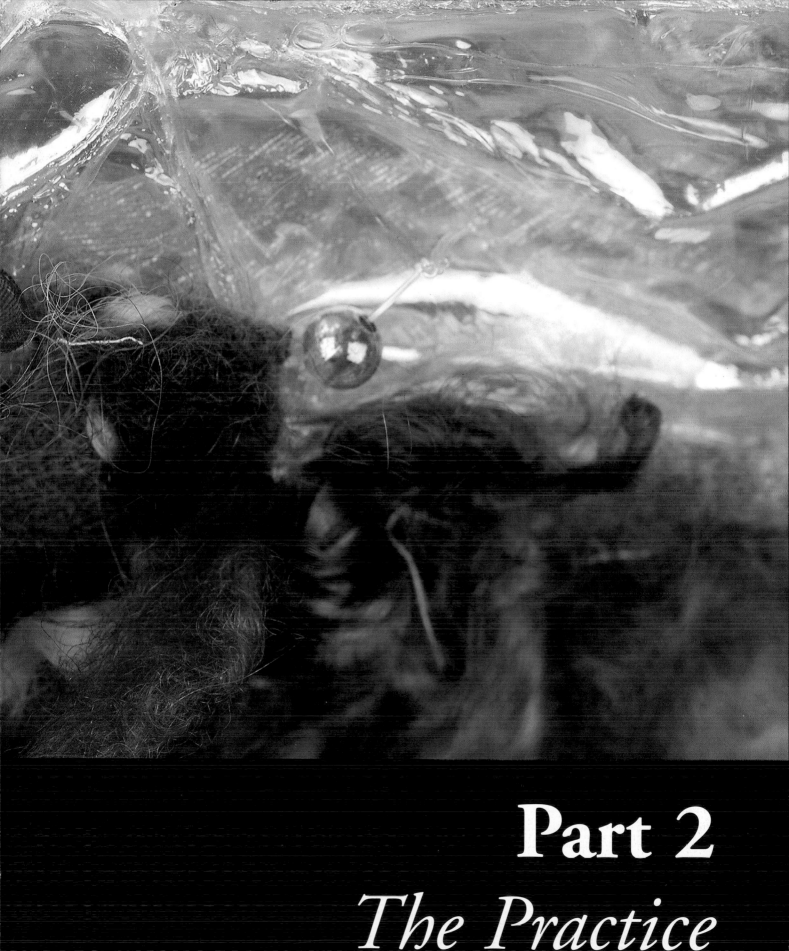

Part 2
The Practice

Bondaweb (Wonder-Under)

Bondaweb (Wonder-Under), or similar products such as fusible web, is a fine web of glue. It is so fine it is double-sided. You may have used it for appliqué in patchwork, quilting or other craft work.

You can also use it to apply heat-transfer foils, threads, flat sequins, grasses, dried or pressed flowers – the list goes on. It makes a wonderful surface for stitch, without stiffening your fabric too much. Because it is double-sided, once you have removed the backing paper from the Bondaweb (Wonder-Under) you must always iron your work with baking parchment on the top and underneath to prevent it sticking to the wrong surface. Once Bondaweb has been painted it is not particularly washable. The fine surface of the web is fragile, and unless sealed will deteriorate with wear. Being beaten to submission in a washing machine with biological powder would most certainly finish it off.

Depending on your finished piece, Bondaweb can be sealed with varnish, acrylic wax, a chiffon scarf or Lamifix.

If you haven't used Bondaweb before, take a piece in your hand and feel it. It has a rough and a smooth side. The smooth side is the backing paper that supports the web. Once you have ironed off your web you will remove this. The rough side is the dangerous side! This is the side you decorate with paint, soft fabric pens or crayons. The web can also be run through an inkjet printer if supported on firm paper (though not a laser printer or photocopier, as they use heat). The web is quite fragile, so try not to be too rough with it.

Pelmet Vilene (Pellon) decorated with painted and foiled Bondaweb (Wonder-Under) and 3D Medium.

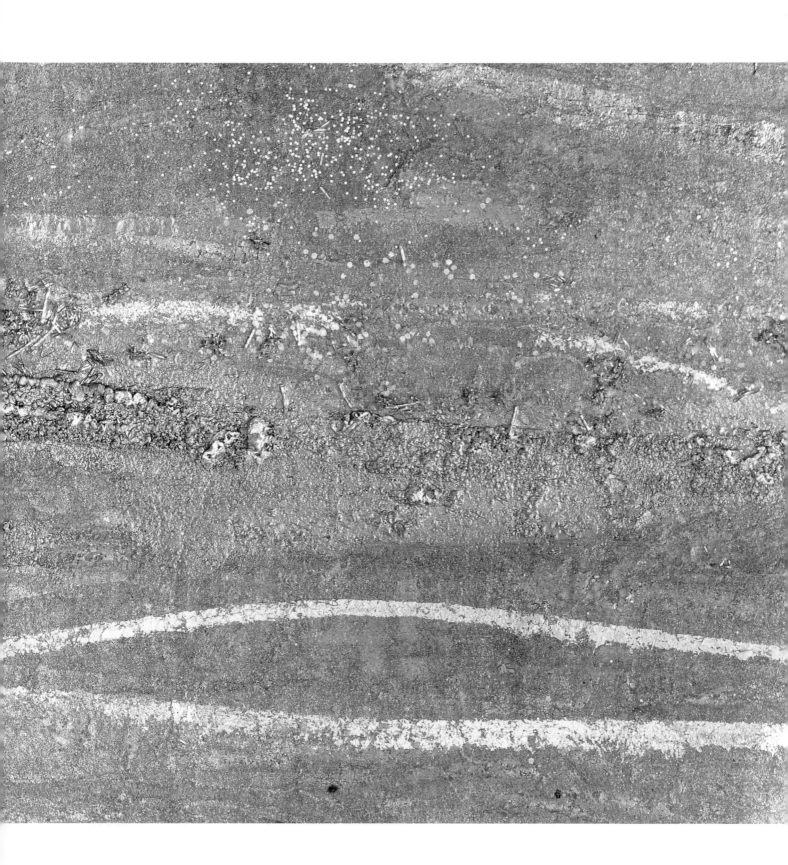

Painting Bondaweb (Wonder-Under)

The materials you will need for this are: newspaper, water-based paints, a 50mm (2in) paintbrush, a water jar, and a dish or plate for mixing paints.

This process takes a long time to dry, so paint it well ahead of when you need it.

Unless you are working on a large-scale project, work with manageably sized pieces of Bondaweb (Wonder-Under). Somewhere between A4 and A3 size is large enough to work with, and easier to store when it's dry.

Lay out the newspaper on a firm, stable work surface. You will need two or three layers of newspaper, as you will be using a lot of water. If you are working on your best table then lay a thick piece of plastic under the newspaper. If you do this a lot you may wish to invest in a cheap plastic tablecloth.

Any water-based paint is suitable for painting Bondaweb, but some are better than others. Watercolour paints don't have enough pigment in them. The colour will be very pale. Try experimenting with inks and dyes.

Choose the colours of paint you want to colour your Bondaweb with. If you are using acrylics then water them down by half. Because you are working with a lot of water the colours will bleed together and look lovely. Apply the paints gently with a wide paint brush on the rough side of the Bondaweb; this saves time and causes fewer disturbances to the fragile web.

If you wish you can brush water onto the web before you start. This gets the paint moving faster. The backing paper will start to ripple and you will get beautiful textured effects. Then you wait for it to dry. The web must be bone-dry before you use it. Try different effects on the web, such as wax crayons and block printing.

Once the web is dry, lay it painted-side down onto your paper or fabric and cover the whole thing with baking parchment. Iron smoothly and continuously for at least a minute with the iron on the cotton setting. Set the iron to one side and wait for your work to cool down. If you try to remove the Bondaweb before it has cooled right down it will peel off the surface you have just ironed it onto.

When the Bondaweb is dry it can be cut into any shape. I would recommend ironing your cut, painted Bondaweb shapes with the backing on and then peeling it off when it has cooled right down. If you want a more abstract effect then try tearing the Bondaweb into pieces. I always take the backing paper off at this point as I like to overlap the web as I work.

Beautiful effects can be achieved with water-based paints on Bondaweb (Wonder-Under). Try using two or three tones of one colour and let the paint bleed together.

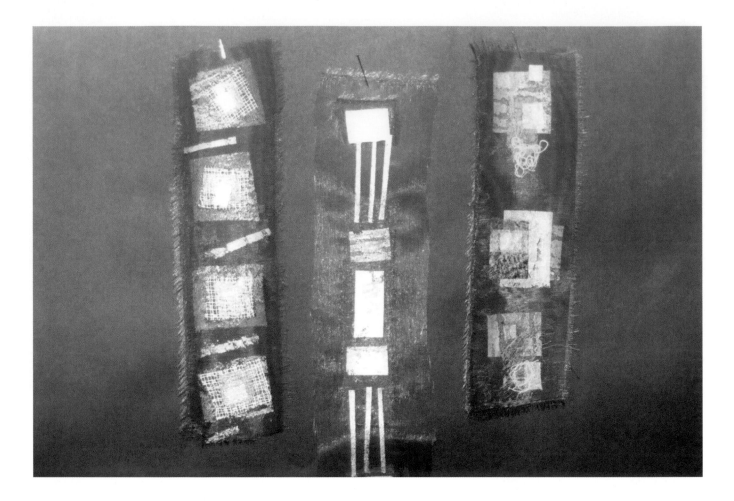

Above: Foiled Bondaweb
(Wonder-Under) samples
by Annie Kemp.

Right: Various wrapping,
printed and handmade
papers torn and bonded
onto a brown paper
background.

Far right: *Torn Shadows* by
Kim Thittichai. Painted
Bondaweb (Wonder-Under)
on handmade paper, with
overlying hand-dyed scrim,
chiffon and paper motifs.

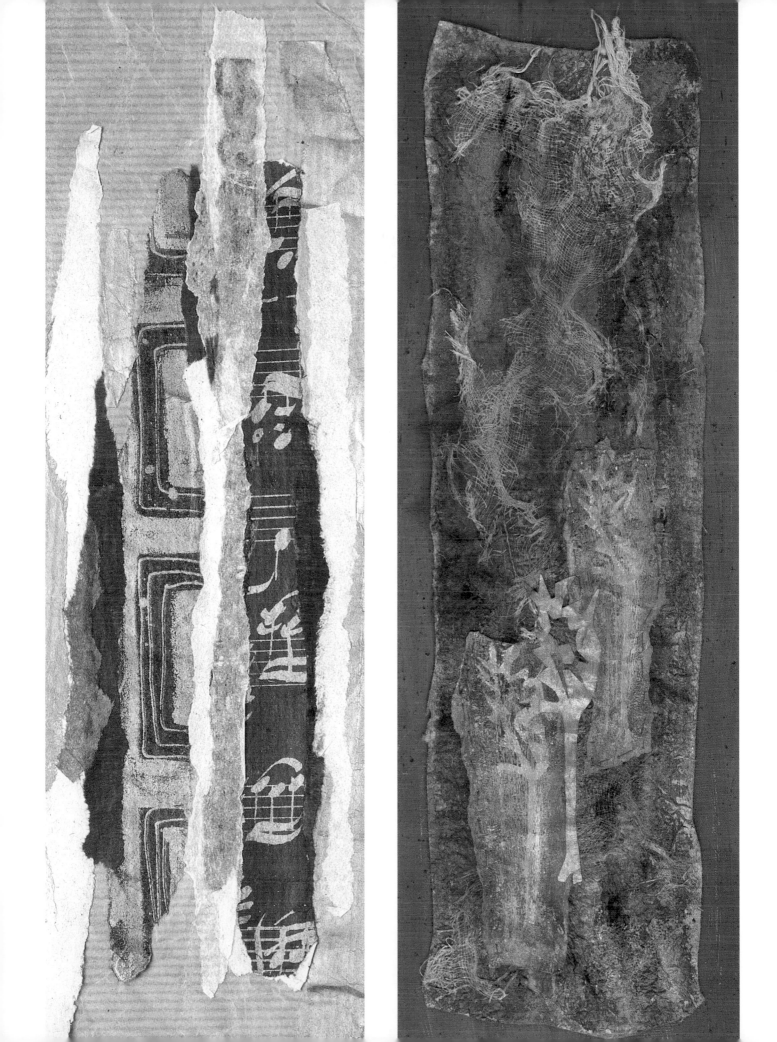

If you are new to using painted Bondaweb (Wonder-Under) as a surface to iron decorations onto, try these experiments:

- Iron the painted Bondaweb (Wonder-Under) onto a variety of papers, including handmade ones.
- Try the same with different fabrics, dark and light, sheer and heavy.
- Try tearing papers and laying them onto painted Bondaweb.
- Decorate polyester organza with painted Bondaweb, then heat gun it.

You can apply all kinds of delightful decorative objects to Bondaweb as long as they are flat and dry. Try grasses, fluffy seeds, skeleton leaves or sequins.

You can create wonderful drifts of colour and texture by using fabric and thread snips, and it is a great way of using up all your odd small pieces of fabric and unwanted lengths of yarn and thread. To create fabric strips, roll four small squares of sheer fabric – around 10cm (4in) square each – into a tight roll, and snip very thin sections off with sharp scissors.

Heat-transfer foils with Bondaweb (Wonder-Under)

Heat-transfer foils will adhere to Bondaweb (Wonder-Under) wherever you apply heat. They need to be placed colour-side up on your work. The foils can be transferred with soldering irons or a flat iron. When using your soldering iron, bear in mind that the tip is very fine, so work slowly. It is not necessary to press hard, since it is the heat that transfers the colour, not the pressure. Using a soldering iron is similar to using a hot pen, so you can draw quite intricate shapes. When using the iron with heat-transfer foils, use the side of the iron for strips and slashes and the flat of the iron to transfer a large area. When using the side of the iron, keep it at a right angle to the table, with the sole plate facing away from your body. You don't need to press hard – just let the heat do the work. Once you have transferred your design just tear off the foil and your design will be revealed.

Brown sample by Ruth Hodge.

The samples (above and opposite) by Ruth Hodge are perfect examples of the joyous effect you can get with painted Bondaweb (Wonder-Under) and heat-transfer foil with a few fabric snips added for good measure.

The red sample (opposite) has various layers and strips of painted Bondaweb applied to black fabric. This gives a fantastic contrast. Pink and blue fabric snips and fluffy threads were then ironed onto the Bondaweb.

The above sample also has the painted Bondaweb on black fabric, with black fabric snips and a very dramatic zigzag of heat-transfer foil, which has been applied with the side of the iron.

Unpainted Bondaweb (Wonder-Under)

Unpainted Bondaweb (Wonder-Under) can be used to apply heat-transfer foil to items that need to be washable. Simply cut your shape from the Bondaweb with the backing paper still attached. I find that when cutting shapes out of Bondaweb, particularly complicated ones, it is best to leave the backing paper on, as it helps support the shape.

If you are making letters or numbers, you may need to reverse your shape. Iron the Bondaweb shape onto your item web-side down, remembering to protect your iron with baking parchment. When the Bondaweb is cold, peel off the backing paper. Take a piece of heat-transfer foil and place colour-side up on top of the Bondaweb shape. Again using baking parchment, iron the foil (on a moderate setting) onto the Bondaweb shape. If the foil starts to pucker it means the iron is too hot. Once the foil is cold, peel it off. You should have a perfect reproduction of the original shape. This finished product is washable because you haven't painted the Bondaweb.

Above: Greetings cards by Angie Hughes. This simple greetings card (left) was made by cutting out a heart from unpainted Bondaweb (Wonder-Under). Offcuts of decorated fabric make fabulous greetings cards (right). Just buy some aperture cards to mount them, and you will never be stuck for a card again.

Wooden mirror frame with Bondaweb (Wonder-Under) decoration

Yes! You can iron onto wood! Providing the surface of the wood is flat – because the sole plate of the iron is flat – there will be no problem. The choice of project is up to you, but I will demonstrate using a wooden mirror frame. The wood needs to be dry, smooth and unvarnished.

Tear the painted Bondaweb (Wonder-Under) into strips and remove the backing paper. Build up your decoration around the frame, overlapping the Bondaweb as you go. Don't try to add all the decoration at once. It is much better to do this in two or three stages. You can always add more.

Once you are happy with your overlapped Bondaweb take your sheet of silicone-coated baking parchment and lay it over the whole area that is to be ironed. Set your iron to the cotton setting and iron with gentle pressure over the area for two minutes, making sure you move the iron continually.

Wait for the baking parchment to cool right down, and then remove it. It will only come away cleanly and easily when it is cold. At this stage you can still add more Bondaweb to build up the colour.

You can now add any threads, papers, plastics, foils, fabrics, dried leaves or other items, as discussed in earlier chapters. Add your decoration sparingly – remember the saying, 'less is more'.

When you have finished decorating your mirror all that is left to do is to seal it. Many different types of varnish and acrylic sealer are commercially available. My personal favourites are acrylic wax or polyurethane varnish. Both can be applied with a paintbrush. The acrylic wax washes out of brushes in water, while the varnish brush needs to be cleaned with white spirit. If your project is going to be handled, it will need to be sealed.

Book cover by Kim
Thittichai. Decorated
with painted Bondaweb
(Wonder-Under), heat-
transfer foils, sequins
and hot-fix crystals.

There are many surfaces that you can iron onto. If you have already tried ironing onto wood, try metal. As long as the surface is dry and flat and won't melt, there should be no problem. Two favourites of mine are Pelmet Vilene (Pellon) and handmade paper. Try applying painted Bondaweb (Wonder-Under) on the covers of hardback books. Why not try making your own slip covers of Pelmet Vilene (Pellon) decorated with this method? One word of warning – don't try to iron onto plastic or glass. The plastic will melt (you might not want it to) and the glass will crack or smash.

This book cover was decorated with painted Bondaweb (Wonder-Under) that was used to adhere sequins and glitter. Hot-fix rhinestones were then added with a Gem Master, and acrylic wax was applied to seal the cover.

Thick white recycled cartridge paper is a very satisfying surface to bond onto. Try painting your paper with spent Procion dyes. Once this is dry, your paper can be printed onto. Experiment with different printing blocks and stamps. Do you prefer metallic to plain paints? Once you have coloured your paper to your liking and it is dry, tear it in half, then tear one of the halves into irregular strips. Take some Bondaweb that you have painted in similar tones. Iron strips of the Bondaweb on the un-torn half of paper. Lay some of the torn strips of paper onto the Bondaweb with the strips all lying in the same direction. Iron this off, not forgetting your baking parchment. Add more Bondaweb and more strips, slowly building up the surface. Other decoration can be added, but keep the colours down to a 'dull roar'. Try seed heads and ripped skeleton leaves for more texture.

Right: Strips of printed
and dyed paper bonded
together and stitched.

This piece was made from all the odd bits of paper I had left over from an earlier project. I keep all 'leftovers' in clear plastic bags and try to organize them into tones of one colour. I can happily spend precious hours coordinating my supplies, and yet never find time to clear up my studio and my work space. I tend to work in a nest of materials, building up more supplies as I go but leaving myself with less and less space to actually work in. 'From chaos comes creativity' is a favourite saying of mine that regularly comes back to haunt me when I can't find a crucial piece of fabric or Tyvek bead. Try to find a balance between enjoying your workspace and being able to find things when you need them.

Torn pieces of handmade paper, some already printed and painted, some plain, have been bonded onto a sheet of handmade paper. Extra Bondaweb (Wonder-Under) was added in a sympathetic colour to adhere small pieces of natural scrim, artichoke heart seeds and black glitter. The whole thing took about an hour to construct. It is one of my favourite pieces.

Tyvek

Tyvek is a fascinating product. It is made from 100 per cent polyester and can be distressed by using heat. It can be ironed between baking parchment or heated and distressed with a heat gun. Tyvek is rip-proof, so you will need to cut it with scissors or a fine-pointed soldering iron. Experiment with different edges.

This material comes in various weights and sizes. A4 sheets – 210 x 297mm (8¼ x 11¾in) – are one of the most popular sizes to work with. Tyvek is sold under various names, but I will just refer to it as 'heavyweight' and 'lightweight'.

Always iron Tyvek between two sheets of baking parchment. When using the iron, don't press heavily. The pebbles or bubbles will need room to develop. Gently run the iron over your work in regular movements and let the heat build up. Start with your iron on medium; you can always turn it up if the Tyvek isn't moving fast enough for you. Keep checking your work to make sure it hasn't disappeared.

Heavyweight Tyvek looks and feels like paper. As it is quite firm it can be fed through an inkjet printer (though not a laser printer or photocopier, as they use heat). It is fascinating to print an image and then distort it, but knowing when to stop can be a problem. Try ironing on one side, then turning it over and ironing again (see sample, opposite). Heavy Tyvek will give you a lovely 'pebble' effect. But remember that you can never get the same effect twice, so don't even try.

Lightweight Tyvek is a softer, more fabric-like product that will give you a less pronounced bubble effect. It has a much more subtle surface when heated than the heavy Tyvek. It can look like rock formations or delicate snakeskin. As the light Tyvek is thinner than the heavy, extra care is needed when heating it. Your work can quickly disappear if you are not careful.

The main problem with Tyvek is … it looks like Tyvek. I know that may sound strange, but along with 3D Medium or Xpandaprint it can be very distracting on a piece of work. The most important thing to remember when working with this wonderfully versatile product is to disguise it. An experimental rectangle of painted Tyvek that has merely been distressed with an iron is probably not going to be good enough to apply to a piece of work. Develop your technique. Twist and shape your Tyvek. Paint it in similar tones to your background so that it doesn't leap out when you look at your work.

All weights of Tyvek can be painted and then stitched into. A reminder: always use water-based colouring media when using heat, as oil-based paints and crayons will give off fumes. I like to paint both sides of the Tyvek, as it will curl up and twist when you heat it, exposing both surfaces.

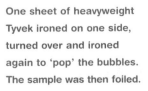

One sheet of heavyweight Tyvek ironed on one side, turned over and ironed again to 'pop' the bubbles. The sample was then foiled.

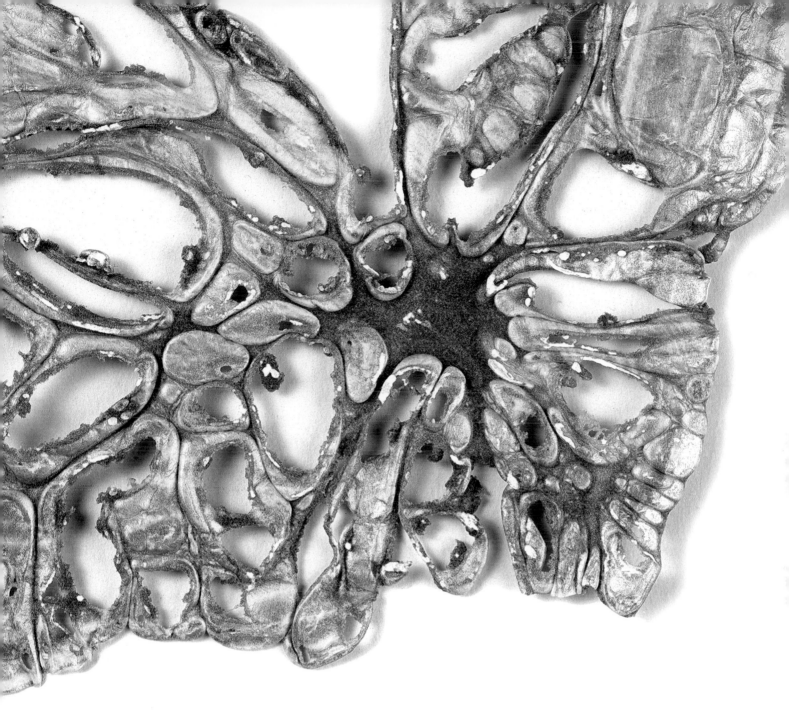

Try the following exercise:
1 Paint a sheet of Tyvek on both sides.
2 When it is dry, place it between two sheets of baking parchment.
3 Turn on your iron to a medium heat.
4 Iron gently over the surface of your work in regular movements for thirty seconds.
5 Check your work to see if it is distorting.
6 If nothing is happening then turn your iron up slightly and try again.
7 You should have a very interesting textured surface. Sometimes you will get pebbles, other times you get holes.
8 If you have gone too far then the Tyvek will become lacy. (This can be a very pretty effect, but can be difficult to catch at this stage before it completely disappears.) Wait till your lacy effect has cooled right down before you peel it off the baking parchment.

Four layers of lightweight
Tyvek, ironed to create
texture and heat-gunned
to exposed different layers.

As a rule, heat-transfer foils should only stick to glue, but if you are lucky they will stick to textured Tyvek with no added glue. Once you have painted and textured your Tyvek, place the heat-transfer foil colour-side up over your work. Place baking parchment over the whole thing and iron over the surface, with firm pressure and smooth movements, for two to three seconds. The iron should be set at moderate for this part of the process. Remove the baking parchment and peel away the heat-transfer foil. The foil should transfer to the Tyvek in a hit-and-miss fashion. Sometimes it just sticks to the ridges, sometimes everywhere – it is by no means an exact science. If the foil does not transfer, try turning up the heat on the iron slightly. Tyvek make fantastic beads – see the section on heat guns (see page 24).

Above left: Lightweight Tyvek, painted and textured with an iron and then foiled.

Above right: A Tyvek bead.

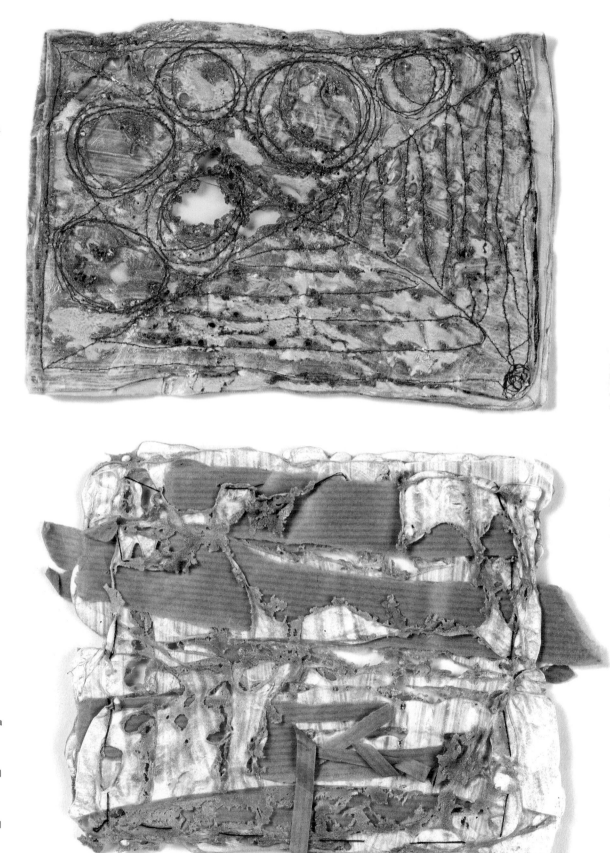

This sample was an experiment to see if stitching heavily into layers of heavy Tyvek retards the way the Tyvek melts when zapped with a heat gun. It does! The stitching restricts how far the Tyvek can curl back.

This sample was an experiment to see what would happen if you layer a natural fibre, in this case brown paper, in between two layers of heavy Tyvek. I found the contrast of the smooth natural brown paper against the distorted Tyvek quite pleasing.

Heavyweight Tyvek can be run through an inkjet printer (not a laser printer or photocopier). Lightweight Tyvek is not suitable for this process unless it is well supported. If in doubt, don't do it.

You never get the same effect twice with Tyvek and you never quite know how it is going to distort. This can obviously be a problem if you are printing words or images onto Tyvek. Try it and see what you think.

The sample bowls on pages 78–79 were experiments to see if I could incorporate synthetic fabrics with heavy Tyvek and still make a three-dimensional piece. Strips of synthetic fabric were machine-stitched to both sides of a sheet of painted heavy Tyvek. The synthetic fabric was lightly heat-gunned to distress it without heating the Tyvek too much. This is because the next stage involved placing the piece between baking parchment and gently ironing to slowly build up the heat and distort the Tyvek. (Gently ironing most synthetic fabrics will only heat them without distorting them.)

While the piece was still very hot it was plunged into a small heat-proof bowl and held there until it was cool. (This part of the process is best done wearing protective gloves, such as suede gardening gloves). The bowls were then hand-stitched, partly as decoration and partly to stop them 'relaxing' and coming apart. The gold bowl on page 79 was a bit flat on the bottom, so I added a little stand.

You can print on acrylic-painted heavyweight Tyvek using an ink-jet printer (opposite). The Tyvek is then heat-gunned and ironed (above).

Right and opposite:
Synthetic fabrics can be
incorporated with heavy
Tyvek to make a three-
dimensional piece.

Combining Tyvek

This lovely little bag by Carrie Donohoe has been decorated with flowers that have been fashioned from lightweight Tyvek. Lightweight Tyvek is quite strong and can be used safely as an embellishment.

Bag by Carrie Donohoe, embroidered with Tyvek flowers.

Disguising Tyvek

This is the first piece of work in a series of three exploring the concept of identity. How is your personal identity constructed? How many layers does it have? How do you define yourself? How does society label you? Individual identity is held together by strings and ideas, interwoven with experiences that make you the person you are.

Heavyweight Tyvek, painted in black and white, was attached to a canvas. A grid of cotton thread was then constructed across the whole canvas to trap various layers of burnt papers, consisting of envelopes, bills and other documents that tell the story of our lives.

Personal Identity by
Jayne Routley.

Pelmet Vilene (Pellon)

Pelmet Vilene (Pellon), and the new Heavy Pelmet Vilene Plus, are invaluable products for creating three-dimensional pieces of work. Pelmet Vilene (Pellon) is a sew-in interfacing used in soft furnishings. Heavy Pelmet Vilene Plus is much heavier, with the added advantage of having Bondaweb (Wonder-Under) on one side. This makes it a very exciting product. Pelmet Vilene can be cut easily with scissors, but Heavy Pelmet Vilene Plus is more easily cut with a craft knife or scalpel. When using knives I would recommend using one with a retractable blade. Failing that, always keep your knives in a strong box with a well-fitting lid. If you use a scalpel keep it safe by slipping a cork onto the end of the blade. Never forget that these blades are extremely sharp – it is very easy to cut yourself on them.

Both types of Pelmet Vilene will take transfer paint and Procion dye as well as paints and Markal sticks. The beauty of the Heavy Pelmet Vilene Plus is that you can dye the adhesive side and it will still be adhesive. Paint seems to 'clog' the adhesive. Try applying threads and foil to the adhesive. It makes a wonderful double-sided, very stiff fabric.

Both types of Pelmet Vilene can be rolled and folded and machine-stitched. The Heavy Pelmet Vilene Plus is so rigid it can stand up by itself. It is the perfect product for making boxes.

Detail from *A Walk in the Park* by Lee Brown.

A Walk in the Park by Lee
Brown is based on scenes
in Gaudí's Guell Park in
Barcelona.

Heavy Pelmet Vilene Plus

Lee Brown is ostensibly a quilt artist; she originally trained at the London School of
Fashion and teaches City and Guilds Patchwork and Quilting in Kent. Lee's main
passion is how to make her work look three dimensional through the use of tonal
value. Her previous subjects have included Gaudí's Sagrada Familia cathedral in
Barcelona and the Riders Gallery in Prague Castle. Lee has used Heavy Pelmet
Vilene Plus for this piece, as it needed to be quite strong. The box measures 80 x 40
x 35cm (31½ x 15¾ x 13¾in). If the box had been constructed in Pelmet Vilene it
would have collapsed.

Having made drawings in Guell Park, Lee was able to refer back to her sketchbook
to design the box. Each corner of the box is a different column, and each side is a
different view in the park. The decoration has been created by drawing directly onto
the plain side of the Heavy Pelmet Vilene Plus using a fine-tipped soldering iron,
giving a fine burnt line. Procion dye has then been painted on to great effect. Lee
and I have attended several summer schools with Ruth Issett, an expert in the use of
Procion dyes, and our confidence in using them, and colour in general, has grown
in leaps and bounds. Do seek out good tutors if you feel at all unsure of any process.
You can only gain from working with others.

The mosaic (left) forms one of the ends of the box. To achieve the mosaic effect, the
shapes were individually cut out and applied to the adhesive side of another piece of
Heavy Pelmet Vilene Plus.

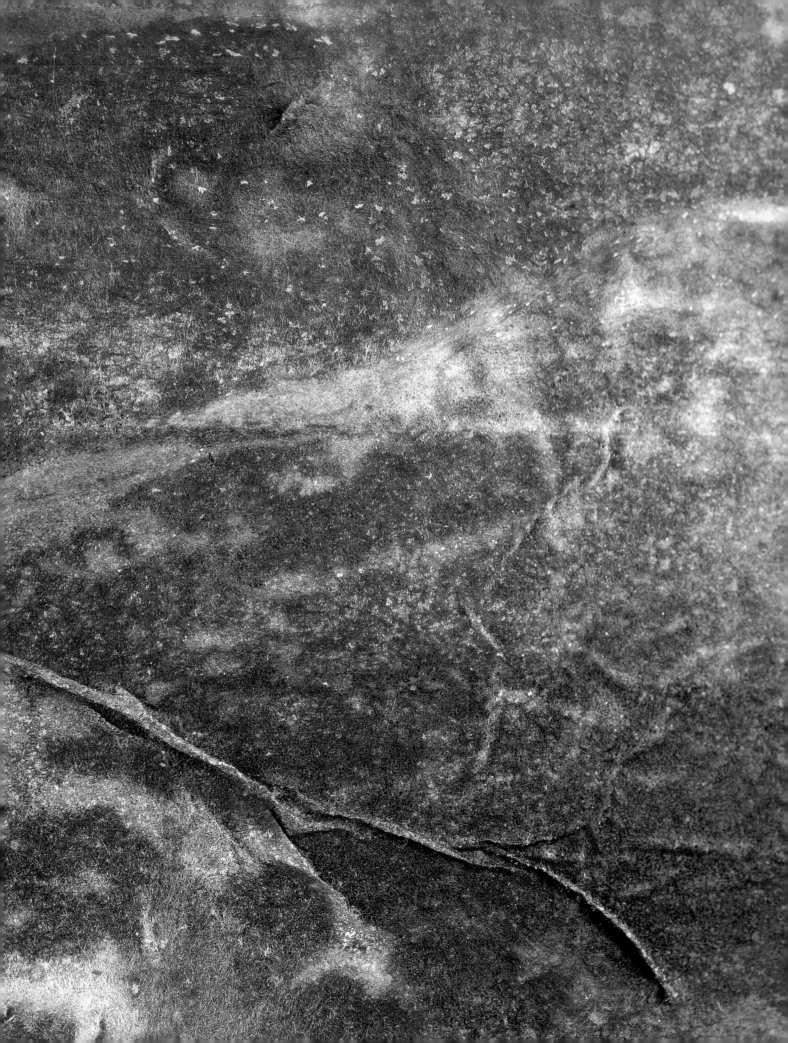

Getting into three dimensions

Having lived in Sussex, UK, for many years now I find I am continually drawn to observing the beauty of the local landscape. I even find the time to paint scenes and colours that move me, though I am not a confident painter. This vessel has been created in response to a particularly beautiful sunset over the South Downs. Trying to portray a scene that has probably been reproduced thousands of times before can be very off-putting. Taking the essence of the scene seemed to be the best way for me to proceed.

This vessel has been constructed from Heavy Pelmet Vilene Plus. This Vilene has a self-adhesive side that can be dyed and still retain its adhesive properties. Hand-dyed silk hankies have been ironed onto the dyed surface, then painted Bondaweb (Wonder-Under) has been applied to 'knock back' the bright colours of the silk.

This surface could be developed further by printing onto it or adding 3D Medium. Maybe a few torn skeleton leaves or similar items would enhance it too.

Of Land, Sea and Sky by Kim Thittichai (right) and close-up detail (left).

Larger Vessels

This vessel is 1.5m (5ft) tall and is constructed from Pelmet Vilene (Pellon). The vessel was made before I was introduced to the Heavy Pelmet Vilene Plus. Even with a steel frame inside the vessel to keep the Pelmet Vilene (Pellon) stretched, the fabric still dips in places.

I love texture. I take photographs of rust, rotten wood, pebbles – whatever I find attractive. This vessel is based on the strata in the cliff of a beach I saw in Cornwall.

To make this piece, Pelmet Vilene (Pellon) was painted with metallic acrylic paint. Large sheets of Bondaweb (Wonder-Under) were then painted in toning metallic colours. Once the Bondaweb (Wonder-Under) was dry, I tore it into several long sections. Removing the backing paper from the painted Bondaweb enabled me to build up layers of colour quickly. The Bondaweb was ironed off with baking parchment. You can easily see from the picture the different layers of colour. To get drifts of texture and interest I first applied artichoke heart seeds to the Bondaweb, then painted 3D Medium around the seeds. When expanding the 3D Medium with a heat gun I had to be careful not to burn the seeds. The 3D Medium was then painted with a mixture of metallic acrylic paint and shoe polish.

This was all very nice but a little dull. It needed something more – though not glitter – so out came the embossing powders. I use the thickest and chunkiest embossing powders I can find. I stick them onto my work with whatever comes to hand – PVA glue, glue stick, Bondaweb, or whatever else might work best for the project I am working on. Embossing powders are not washable, so as long the powders don't blow away when you heat them you can use any sticky media you like. Once the embossing powder is molten I like to add extra pinches of variously coloured powders. This is a little bit wasteful, but you do get a wonderfully organic effect. Embossing powders give a sheen and a shine to your work where glitter and heat-transfer foil can sometimes be a bit too flashy.

Strata by Kim Thittichai (see pages 88–89 for a close-up detail).

Brooch project

Materials required:
Pelmet Vilene (Pellon)
Acrylic paint
Bondaweb (Wonder-Under)
Heat-transfer foil
A needle and strong thread
A brooch pin
Dimensional paint
Acrylic wax or varnish

Method:

1 Cut the Pelmet Vilene (Pellon) into two pieces, one for the brooch front and one for the back. Paint both pieces with metallic acrylic paint. Put one piece aside for the brooch back.

2 Apply strips of Bondaweb (Wonder-Under) to the remaining piece of Pelmet Vilene. Once these have cooled, remove the backing paper and apply heat-transfer foils in whatever colour combination you see fit.

3 Cut out two matching shapes, one from each piece of Pelmet Vilene.

4 Sew the brooch pin on the painted side of the brooch back.

5 Cut a piece of Bondaweb the same size and shape as your brooch, to glue your brooch pieces together. Remove the backing paper and place it between the front and back brooch pieces. Making sure that the right sides face out.

6 Place the brooch front side down onto baking parchment and iron the whole brooch, taking care to iron around the brooch pin using another sheet of baking parchment to protect the back of the brooch. The brooch should be firmly stuck together.

7 Now the fun begins. Decorate your brooch with whatever you fancy. I have used dimensional paint. You could try sequins or hot-fix gems.

8 When you have finished decorating your brooch, seal it with acrylic wax or varnish for durability.

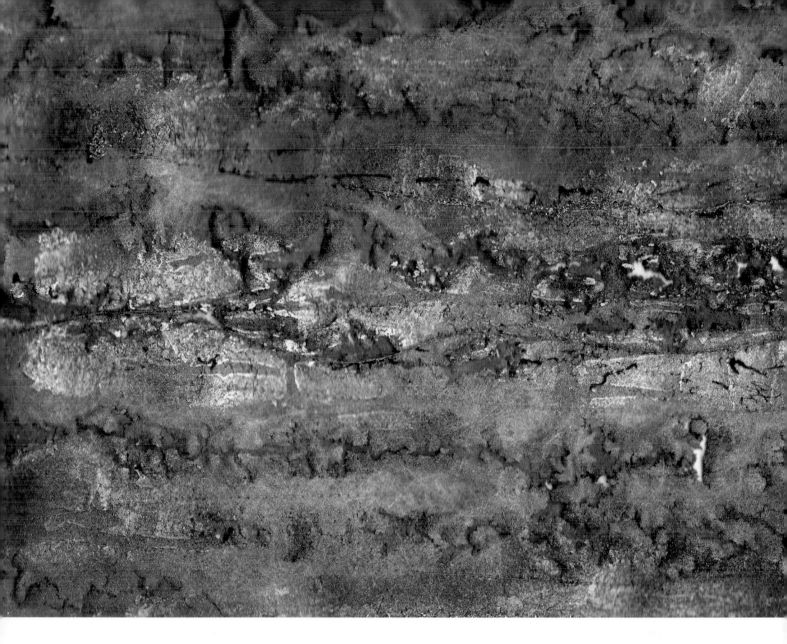

Two layers of heavyweight Lutradur stitched together. Painted Bondaweb (Wonder-Under) was applied to the top layer in torn strips and the sample was heat-gunned to reveal the bottom layer. Because the Lutradur has a matt surface it creates a wonderful crusty effect.

Lutradur

Lutradur is a spun-bonded non-woven fabric that comes in various weights. The lightweight version is used by florists to wrap flowers. Because of the way it is manufactured the thinner weights are quite lacy and are great for overlaying and zapping through with a heat gun. The heavyweight material pictured here would be very suitable for projects that need strength. Though not as heavy as Pelmet Vilene (Pellon), it is still very useful for transfer printing, painting and thoroughly having a good time. Lutradur can be treated the same way as Pelmet Vilene (Pellon), but has the added advantage of being synthetic, so it can be heat-gunned. A soldering iron will slice through Lutradur like a hot knife through butter, giving an excellent sealed edge.

Plastic and Cellophane

Detail of one of the *Crazy Vessels* by Sarah Hawkins (for the whole bowl see page 103).

There is something very satisfying about recycling. The redemptive quality of using everyday materials by using them to create crazy or even beautiful work can't help but make you feel good. And the materials are free!

There is one main difference between plastic and cellophane. Plastic will stick to itself and cellophane won't. Both can be moulded when hot, but plastic retains its heat more effectively, so be very careful when handling plastic to leave it a few minutes after it has been heated – I would recommend wearing suede gardening gloves when handling it. Using an iron to shape your work will give you a flat surface, as the iron plate itself is flat. If you want something more three dimensional then use the heat gun. The heat gun is also useful for distressing cut edges.

I started using plastic bags and foil packaging early on in my teaching career. As usual there was virtually no budget for the class, so I had to cast around to find ideas for supplies. My students and I used thin strips of brightly coloured plastic shopping bags to weave and stitch into rug canvas. Using bodkin needles with very large eyes the students were able to create amazing layered textures using donated knitting yarns alongside the plastic strips.

While walking across the playground of the same school after lunch one day, my eye was caught by something pink and sparkly on the ground. It was a prawn cocktail crisp packet (this was when crisp manufacturers had just started combining foil with plastic in their packaging). I collected all the shiny crisp packets I could find and washed them, and the students had a great time sorting them into colours. The packets were then cut up into squares and used for mosaic. Whenever I worry about not having enough supplies or money for the latest materials, I think back to those days. It is so easy to pick up the phone and flex your credit card. But look around you first; see what useful things you can find.

Getting organized

Always try to sort out your materials before you start. Separate plastic from foil and from cellophane. If you can sort and store your materials in separate bags it will be much easier to find just what you want when you need it. Plastics and cellophane tend to 'spread', so make sure you have a clear work space before you start to work. Your recycling boxes will have a lot less in them in future.

Always wash any packaging that has had food in it. The cellophane sleeves that greetings card are sold in are very useful pockets to laminate seeds and other small items in. Old and torn clear plastic sleeves that are no longer used for keeping papers in are also very useful. Plastic drinks bottles can be heat-gunned to great

effect. And as for all the chocolate wrappers and crisp packets – these can be melted with an iron and heat-gunned to your heart's content. If you don't eat chocolate I'm sure your friends will save their wrappers for you.

Seeds laminated between two sheets of cellophane.

Cello-Foil

This product is generally used by florists to wrap flowers. It is manufactured in many colours and is silvered on the reverse side. It has a high metallic shine and responds quickly to heat. Iron between baking parchment for wonderful textures. Cello-Foil can also be manipulated with a heat gun.

Cellophane

Although cellophane will not stick to itself, it does pucker and pleat around itself, so will hold together with a little encouragement. It is possible to trap small items, seed heads, fabric and thread snips inside three or four layers of cellophane. This can then be shaped by reheating it.

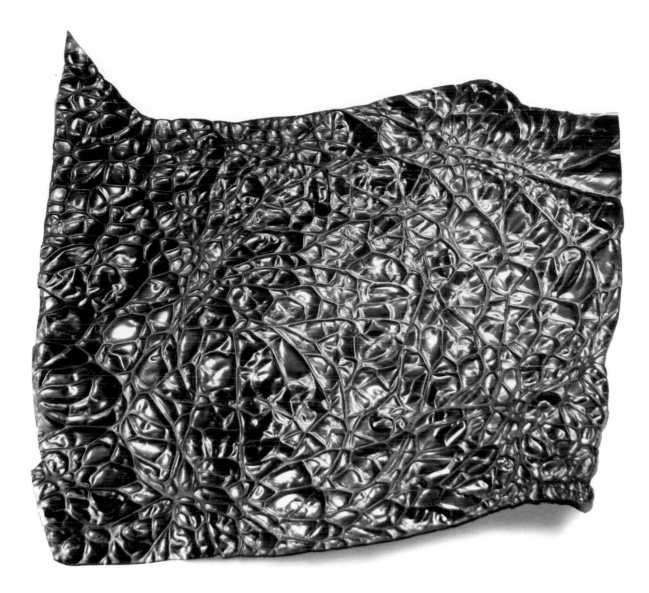

Distressed Cello-Foil.

Plastic bags

Try weaving strips of plastic bags onto a grid and melting it with an iron. Plastic grid can be bought at DIY stores or your local hardware shop; builders' plastic fencing is particularly effective because it is made in bright colours. This can be bought from a builders' merchants by the roll, but if you know a local builder he may sell you a metre or two. Building up thick textures in this way makes a very strong waterproof material. Unfortunately, plastic bags are not lightfast, and the colour will fade quite dramatically if left outside for any length of time.

Magic film

This clear, heat-soluble film is great fun to experiment with. It has been created to make it easier to machine embroider into fabrics with raised fibres such as velvet or towelling. However, it does have other uses. Cut a manageable-sized piece of magic film and paint on it using a water-based paint. When the paint is dry, try distressing parts of the film with a heat gun or an iron. Exciting textures can be developed using this product. When using the iron to dissolve magic film don't forget to use baking parchment.

Left: Tufty bowl by Kim Thittichai. Cellophane moulded over a heat-proof bowl and ironed. Decorated with nylon filament and feathers.

Above: Jumper knitted with video tape by Nadya Derungs.

Next page: A selection of colourful shopping bags, layered and melted together.

Why not try ...?

- Painting clear cellophane or polythene with acrylic paint before you heat-distress it.
- Seeing how many layers of plastic bag you can iron together before you have to start ironing both sides.
- Grating wax crayons melted onto clear polythene or cellophane, then heat-distressing it.
- Layering Cello-Foil with clear cellophane. They will need to be stitched together as they will not bond together.
- Sprinkling glitter in between layers of clear cellophane and then heating with an iron between sheets of baking parchment.

The images on this page have been shaped with an iron. The clear cellophane bowl (opposite) was created by laying three sheets of cellophane onto baking parchment. Another sheet of baking parchment was placed over the cellophane. Using a moderate setting, the iron was used to heat the cellophane and texture it. You can do the same thing – once you are happy with the texture on your piece you can shape it. This is done with two stackable heat-proof bowls. Heat the cellophane between baking parchment, again quickly with the iron, and while it is still hot quickly push it into one of the bowls, placing the other bowl on top to hold the cellophane in place.

There are several things to think about with this process. The cellophane still needs to be hot when you pick it up so I would recommend wearing a suede gardening glove on the hand you are going to push the cellophane into the bowl with. The iron needs to be put down very quickly and safely so make sure your surface is clear of unnecessary stray objects. You need to be aware of where the centre of the bowl should be when you push the cellophane into the bowl, otherwise your piece will be lopsided. This all sounds very complicated, but with practice you will soon get into a smooth working process.

The crazy jumper (above left) was knitted by Nadya Derungs as part of her final project when she took my experimental textiles course. Videotape was knitted into a basic jumper shape, and then red synthetic fabric was woven in a spiral through the front of the jumper. It was then ironed and heat-gunned to distress it.

Using plastic bags

Alison Hermon creates exquisite dresses from the lowly plastic bin liner, occasionally adding plastic carrier bags and cellophane as highlights.

Her work is based on memories from her childhood, reproducing in beautiful detail the clothes that she and her family have worn. Her mother's wedding dress and veil, her first dress from Biba, and her first tutu.

All of Alison's work is produced in her kitchen at the ironing board, with an iron, baking parchment, and piles of plastic bin liners and carrier bags. It is a very basic process used thoughtfully and very creatively. Alison proves that you don't have to use very complicated techniques or materials to produce amazing work. You just need to have a good idea and know how to use your materials to their best advantage.

Left: *Pink Flower Tutu* by Alison Hermon. Melted plastic bin liners can be made into beautiful objects.

Right: *The Wedding Dress* by Alison Hermon. This stunning piece is a plastic replica of Alison's mother's wedding dress.

Using plastic packaging

This dress was created for an exhibition based on maternity. The artist explained:

'My children have all flown the nest now but I can still remember how I was totally immersed in the world of motherhood and its associated responsibilities.

Although I loved being a mum, the maternal instinct took over and the needs of my children became paramount. It was easy to lose myself for a while in this maternal cocoon. *Mummyfied* tries to capture some of the feelings I had at the time. Being wrapped in the all-encompassing world of babies, with the maternity dress, the bulge and the endless nappies.'

Plastic nappy wrappers were ironed onto both sides of a chicken wire dress form, which was moulded to create the 'bump'. Lyn Leese is a member of the Brighton textile artists' groups Necrotex and Angelico.

Mummyfied by Lyn Leese.

Layering plastics

Sarah Hawkins' work has always had a vibrancy and style of its own, making connections between her environment and her work. This range of vessels was created in response to a project set at college. The brief was for the students to develop one three-dimensional piece in materials of their own choice. Sarah created two, both very different and quite crazy, but in their way very beautiful. The bowl (below) has been constructed from a combination of bubble pack, cellophane and plastic. Small beads have been added for extra decoration. The vessel featured on the next page has been created from the very cheap and thin black-and-white striped bags you are given at local markets.

The bowl and vessel have both been moulded by draping the material over shapes and using an iron, then distressed further with a heat gun. Sarah Hawkins is a member of the Brighton-based textile artists' groups Necrotex and Angelico.

Crazy Vessels by Sarah Hawkins.

This stunning vessel (opposite and detail, above) by Sarah Hawkins was created by melting very thin plastic shopping bags with an iron. Further texture is added with a heat gun.

Combining textures

This piece of work was Hazel's final project at the end of her first year. While working on her scrapbook Hazel had found a photograph of a magnificent jellyfish in an old copy of *National Geographic* magazine. To create her piece the body of the jellyfish cellophane was moulded over a large sphere with an iron, then folded over to create the correct shape. The tentacles are a mixture of knitting and embroidery yarns, heat-gunned strips of synthetic fabric and ribbons and plastic bags.

The Jellyfish by Hazel Ranger (left) and close-up detail (opposite).

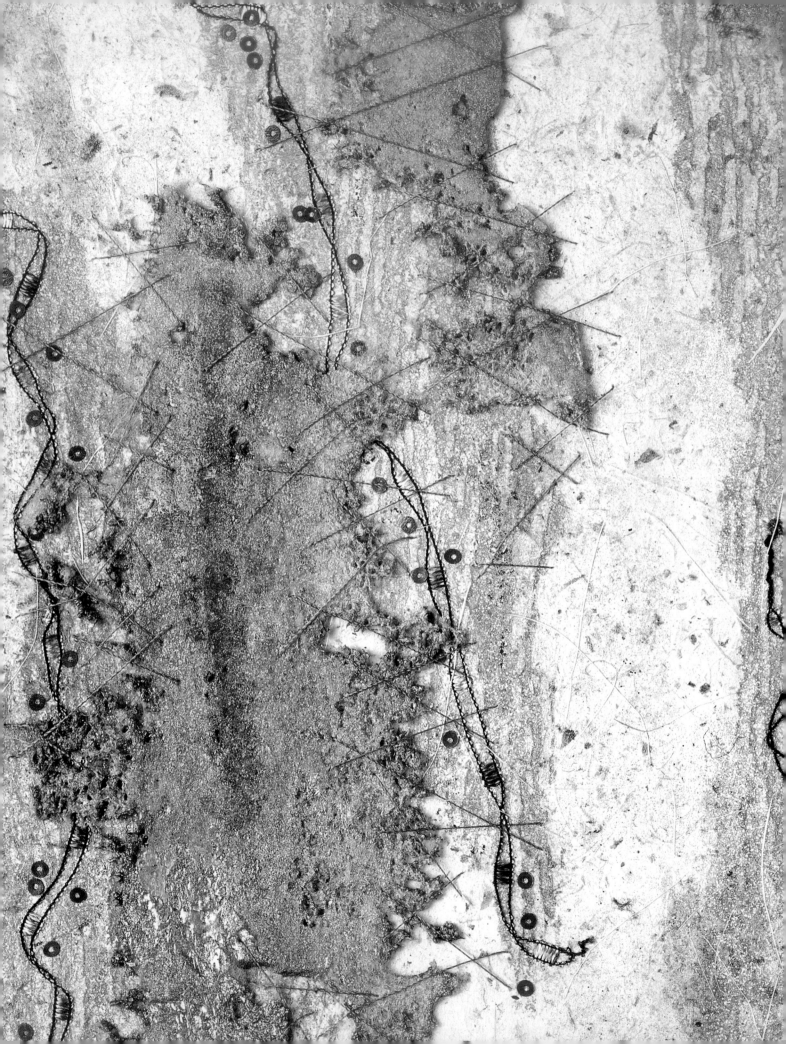

Layered Techniques

Layering materials is great fun but you need to be careful not to have too much variety of texture or colour on the same piece of work. The general rule is that if you are working with a lot of texture, keep the range of colours small, or even limit yourself to tones of one colour. If you want to work in lots of different colours then keep the texture to a minimum – the brain can only cope with so much information. Use natural threads and yarns to stitch your material together. If you use synthetic threads they are likely to melt when you use a heat gun and your work will fall apart.

There are four layers in this sample:
1 Rough handmade paper decorated with toning painted Bondaweb (Wonder-Under).
2 Kunin felt decorated with painted Bondaweb (Wonder-Under) and embossing powders and then heat-gunned.
3 Tiny sequins and threads applied to the painted Bondaweb (Wonder-Under).
4 Large herringbone stitch in toning thread to finish.

Exercise 1

Try layering alternately four or five sheets of heavyweight and lightweight Tyvek. Paint both sides in contrasting colours. Stitch them together and zap with the heat gun to expose different layers in different areas.

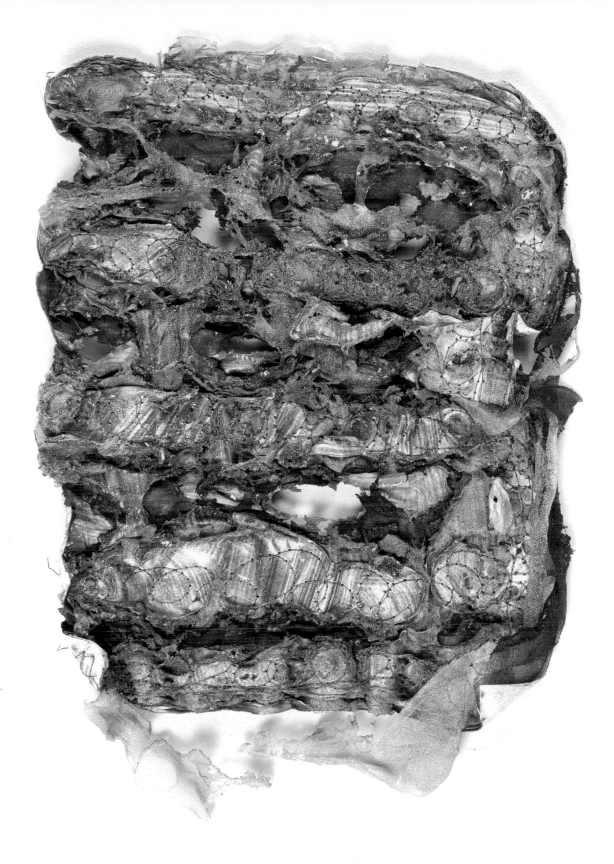

Exercise 2

Try layering polyester organza with Tyvek. Stitch three or four layers together and heat-gun through to different layers. You can make a feature of the hand or machine stitch or just do something basic to hold it all together.

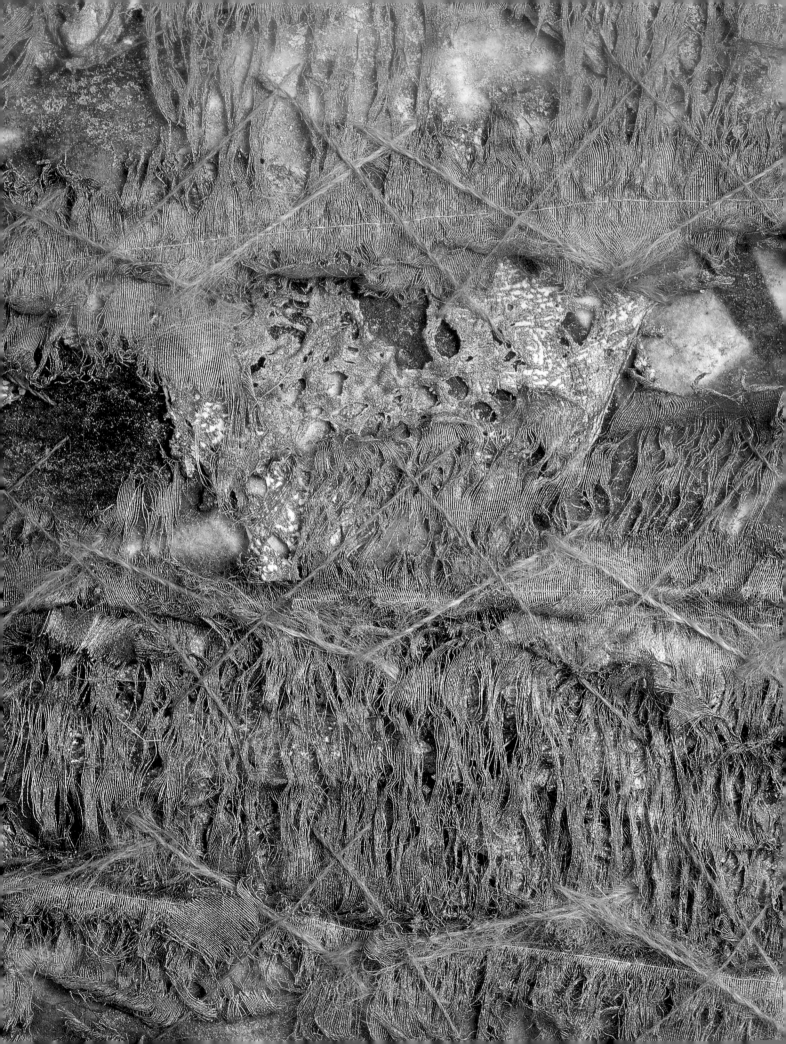

Exercise 3

Try layering clear plastic that has been transfer printed. Cutting these layers with a soldering iron will create a lovely piece of work. Experiment by machine- or hand-stitching into your plastic. You could also try layering colours of sheer fabrics between layers of clear plastic. Try to use colours of a similar tone otherwise the results can be overwhelming.

There are five layers in this sample:
1 Transfer printed Pelmet Vilene (Pellon).
2 Painted Bondaweb (Wonder-Under).
3 Heat-treated Tyvek.
4 Heat-distressed polyester organza.
5 A large-scale herringbone stitch.

Layering paper

There are five layers in this sample:

1 Bark cloth decorated with painted Bondaweb (Wonder-Under) for toning.

2 Gold-painted papers torn and bonded onto the bark cloth.

3 More strips of toning Bondaweb (Wonder-Under).

4 Heavily decorated thick handmade paper torn into strips.

5 Black glitter, threads and 3D Medium.

Dark Landscape by Kim Thittichai.

Leaf by Kim Thittichai.

Blurring edges

There are six layers in this sample:

1 Faux suede fabric decorated with painted Bondaweb (Wonder Under).
2 Skeleton leaf.
3 Thin strips of painted Bondaweb (Wonder-Under) applied over the leaf to 'loose the edges'.
4 Toning threads, heat-transfer foil and fabric snips.
5 Herringbone stitch in natural thread to finish.
6 A coating of three layers of acrylic wax.

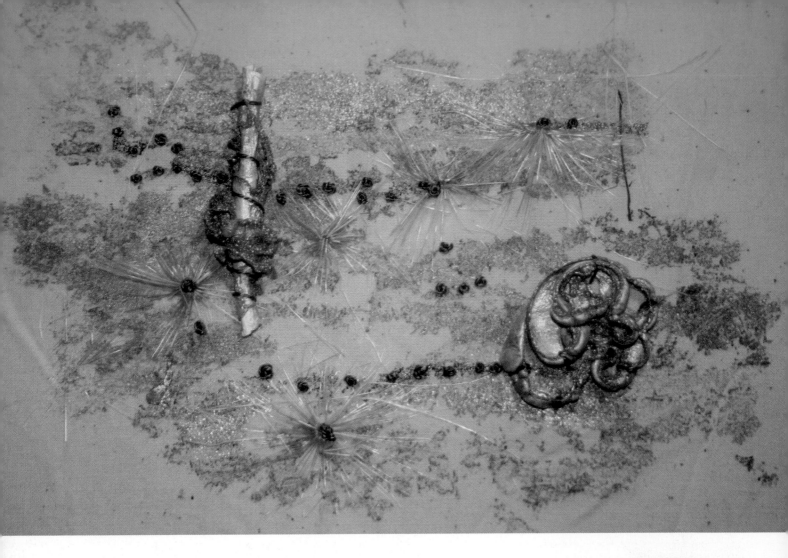

Disguising Tyvek

This sensitive sample (above) was created during Liz's first year at college. We were looking at ways of incorporating Tyvek into students' work. If the Tyvek and Bondaweb (Wonder-Under) are painted the same colour the whole piece will blend together.

The layers used for this piece include:
1 Calico decorated with strips of painted Bondaweb (Wonder-Under).
2 Heat-transfer foil, glitter and seeds applied to the Bondaweb (Wonder-Under).
3 Tyvek beads applied with toning thread.
4 French knot embroidery in toning natural thread.

Using texture

This wall hanging (right) was inspired by the mythical figure of the Green Man. It is a perfect example of using a lot of texture in tones of one colour. To create this piece Alison used many techniques and materials. It is always a popular piece at exhibitions whenever it is hung.

Above: *Cream sample* by
Liz Holford.

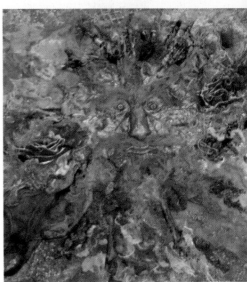

Above: *The Green Man* by
Alison Chesman. Created
using silk fibres, Tyvek beads
and manipulated fabrics.

Susie's Book by Carrie
Donohoe.

Combining Tyvek with machine embroidery

Carrie creates beautiful jewellery, bags and book covers. She specializes in machine
embroidery onto heat- and water-soluble fabrics. The decoration on *Susie's Book* was
made by free machining into vanishing muslin. The vanishing muslin was then
removed with the heat of an iron between baking parchment. The flowers are
constructed from lightweight Tyvek and decorated with glass beads.

From concept to finished piece

Jan was a student with me for four years and was the kind of student all tutors wish for. Being a newcomer to textiles she was at first quiet and hesitant, gradually becoming more confident and producing beautiful and sensitive work.

The piece *Turned to Stone* was inspired by a photograph of petrified tree trunks. Jan worked on various layered samples to decide how best to interpret her idea.

The finished piece was one of my favourites of her final year. Jan's piece was a perfect example of working through the stages from the original idea to final interpretation via drawing and experimental samples.

Faux suede was transfer printed with handmade printing blocks. Polyester chiffon was lightly bonded onto the suede. The chiffon was then heat-gunned. The central panel was finished with a variety of running stitches and black Xpandaprint. The sides of the panel are faux suede decorated with painted Bondaweb (Wonder-Under). The whole thing was then stretched over a frame.

Turned to Stone by Jan Eldridge (left) and pages from her sketchbook (right).

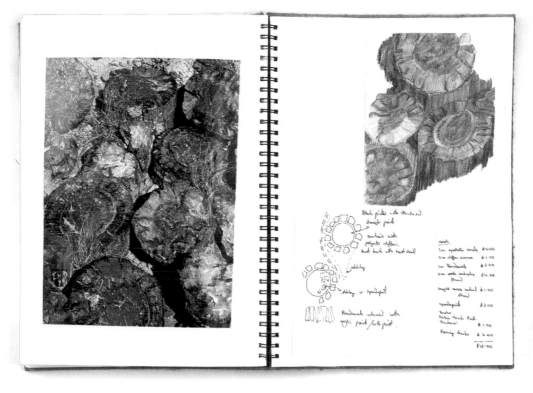

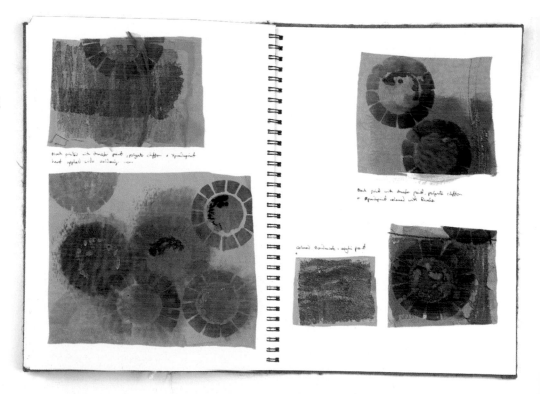

Winter Chill by Wendy Dolan (left) and close-up detail (above).

Using thicker texture

Wendy Dolan specializes in machine embroidery and creative stitching techniques. Wendy trained in art and textiles while studying in Brighton, following with a Diploma in Creative Stitched Textiles a few years later. As a member of the Society of Designer Craftsmen, the Sussex Guild of Designers and Makers and the Embroiderers' Guild Wendy travels all over the UK and is on the Crafts Council Makers' Index. She takes her inspiration from the South Downs, which she lives close to. Other themes and images she explores include fish, ancient relics, architecture and natural landforms.

A variety of cotton fabrics are pieced, patched and layered, then worked into with hand and machine-stitching. Nappy liners are applied, and Xpandaprint is sponged onto the fabric to create more texture. A hot air gun is worked over the surface before painting the design with Sericol fabric inks. Further embellishment and detail is added with machine and hand stitching.

Combining Bondaweb (Wonder-Under) with machine embroidery

With a background in print and design Angie studied City and Guilds creative embroidery at Malvern Hills College where she won the Charles Henry Foyle Trust Award for stitched textiles. Angie went on to study with Liz Harding at GLOSCAT, taking the HNC in stitched textiles.

Angie has started Ledbury Artplace with fellow artist Jeanette McCulloch, where they both teach a variety of workshops.

For the bag (opposite), cotton velvet has been decorated with foiled Bondaweb (Wonder-Under) and machine-stitched with metallic thread. Angie applies the heat-transfer foil by gently heating the Bondaweb and then presses the foil on by hand in patches while the Bondaweb is still warm, slowly building areas of different colours. The bag is then lined and finished with a tassel.

Angie creates wonderful glistening surfaces with Bondaweb (Wonder-Under), heat-transfer foils and machine stitch.

An experimental sample combining Bondaweb (Wonder-Under), machine embroidery and foils.

Finishing Off

To sparkle or not to sparkle? That is the question.

Shimmering Bag by Angie
Hughes.

There are so many different ways of embellishing our work. So many lovely shiny things to stick or sew on. But how much is too much? This is definitely a case of less is more. Adding any kind of sequin, mirror or heat-transfer foil to your work will automatically draw the eye and should be used very sparingly.

While I am just as guilty as the next person of hoarding wonderful beads, sequins, glitter and gems, I use them rarely. Only use them if you are sure they are not going to detract from your work.

Another thing to think about when finishing off your work is how it is going to be hung – or is it going to stand? Will it be glazed in a frame or stuck to a canvas? If it is a wall hanging, how will you clean it?

In my experience, work sells better if it is under glass, though there is no reason for this to be so: you can clean wall hangings with a vacuum cleaner, using a pop sock over the soft-furnishings fitting. Work that is on a canvas can be sealed with acrylic wax or varnish.

I really dislike glazing my work, since I feel it loses something with a pane of glass in the way. However, sometimes it is unavoidable.

And Finally ...

Where do ideas come from? It is a great help to keep a sketchbook or scrapbook going. Add photographs torn from Sunday supplements, articles from newspapers, or postcards from exhibitions – whatever gets you excited. Look at all types of art.

My favourites are the painter Patrick Heron, the colourful glass artist Dale Chihuly and the astonishing sculptor Anish Kapoor. Any art form can inspire, from ceramics and fashion to music and gardening.

With the advent of the internet and ever more sophisticated search engines it has never been easier to research any artist, anywhere in the world. We are living in very exciting times.

Exhibitions are a wonderful way to keep in touch with what and who is up and coming in the textile world. The first exhibition that had a major effect on me was *Under Construction: Exploring Process in Contemporary Textiles* at Brighton Polytechnic in 1996. The seven artists featured included Polly Bins, Caroline Broadhead and Michael Brennand-Wood. The memory of their work is still fresh in my mind now: it changed the way I felt about everything I had done thus far in my life. You may never feel that way about an exhibition, but if you don't go, you never will!

There is an excellent selection of magazines available for anyone interested in textiles. Please see the list at the back of the book. Magazines are a marvellous resource, with plenty of interesting articles on current and historical techniques and methods. They are a great way of finding out where exhibitions are being shown where tutors are teaching, and they are always full of good ideas.

There are many good tutors all over the country, and with the internet it has never been easier to find them. While reading and using books is a useful tool it can never replace the experience of working with and being inspired by an innovative tutor. Go on one-day workshops and summer schools, or evening classes if they run in your area. Form your own groups. There is a splendid contacts facility online at Maggie Grey's quarterly textile review *Workshop on the Web* (www.workshopontheweb.com) to enable people to get together.

Look around you and take some photographs. Photography is a marvellous way of learning composition. Where do you put the point of interest in the frame? Draw your surroundings. It doesn't matter how good or bad your

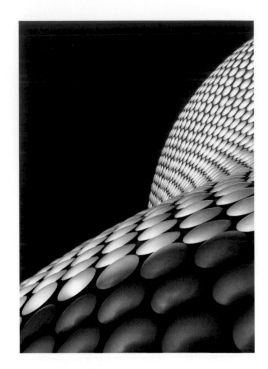

Selfridges building at the Bull Ring in Birmingham, UK.

Anchor at Mevagissy in Cornwall, UK.

Panels painted by my students as a resource for generating designs.

drawings are, the most important thing is that you are looking hard at something in order to draw it. If you belong to a creative group, have a regular drawing session. These panels were painted in a still-life session at college. The still life consisted of large plants, big vases, parasols and odd pieces of furniture and drapery. The students were very nervous to start with but really enjoyed the session by the end; every student ended up producing several drawings and paintings. As the course progressed, sections of the still-life work were used for printing blocks, colour schemes and general inspiration.

Try lots of different media until you find what you feel most comfortable with, be it wax crayons, pastels or paint. While it is a great help to be able to draw, if you find it difficult there are many ways of using and transferring designs. Designs can be generated from the simplest ideas. Just make sure they are your own ideas!

We are living in the most exciting time for textiles. Breaking boundaries has never been so exciting – there is something for everyone.

… you have permission to play!

Contact Information

Suppliers

nid-noi.com
Tel: 01273 698112
Email: info@nid-noi.com
Website: www.nid-noi.com
Pelmet Vilene (Pellon), Heavy Pelmet
Vilene Plus, Lutradur, Tyvek, Cello-Foil,
Lamifix, play packs, threads.

Ario
Tel: 01792 529092
Tel: 01792 429849
Email: fiona@ario.co.uk
Website: www.ario.co.uk
Fusible film, 3D Medium, transfer paints,
Bondaweb (Wonder-Under), glitter, vanishing
muslin, bark cloth and much more.

Ivy House Studio
Tel: 01502 740414
Email: ivyhousestudio@hotmail.com
Website: www.ivyhousestudio.com
Embroidery and surface design supplies.

Margaret Beal
Tel: 01264 365102
Email: burningissues@margaretbeal.co.uk
Soldering irons, polyester organza.

Winifred Cottage
Tel: 01252 617667
Email: sales@winnifredcottage.co.uk
Website: www.winifredcottage.co.uk
Kunin felt, Bondaweb (Wonder-Under),
machine embroidery supplies.

Art Van Go
Tel: 01438 814946
Email: art@artvango.com
Website: www.artvango.co.uk
350 watt heat guns and everything else you
could desire.

Rainbow Silks
Tel: 01494 862111
Email: caroline@rainbowsilks.co.uk
Website: www.rainbowsilks.co.uk
An Aladdin's cave of supplies

Tonertex
Tel: 020 8444 1992
Email: info@tonertex.com
Website: www.tonertex.com
Heat-transfer foils and glitter

Lazertran Ltd
Tel: 01545 571149
Email: mic@lazertran.com
Website: www.lazertran.com
Fantastic image-transfer papers
for any surface.

Patsy May
Website: www.patsymay.co.uk
Heat-transfer foils by the metre.

Rhinestonesonline
Tel: 07757 248793
Website: www.rhinestonesonline.co.uk
Email: Lizzie@RhinestonesOnline.co.uk
A dazzling selection of hot-fix rhinestones.

Whaley's (Bradford) Ltd
Tel:01274 576718
Email: info@whaleys-bradford.ltd.uk
Website: www.whaleys-bradford.ltd.uk
Acetate satin and other fabrics.

Elm Tree Workshop
Tel: 01449 740211
Clover irons.

Paper Cellar
Website: www.papercellar.com
Wonderful sequins and sparkles to iron
on to Bondaweb (Wonder-Under).

Textile groups

PSG (Practical Study Group)
Website: www.practicalstudygroup.co.uk
The PSG is a diverse group of well-qualified,
nationally and internationally renowned textile
artists and tutors. Ruth Issett can be contacted
through the PSG website.

62 group
Website: www.62group.org.uk
The Sixty Two Group of Textile Artists is an
organisation promoting textile art in major
national and international venues.

Threads
Website: www.threads.org.uk
An exciting collaboration by 10 accomplished
textile artists, sharing their passion for exploring
and experimenting with all things textile.

Necrotex
Website: www.necrotex.org.uk
The theme of the exhibition is the use of textiles
for the celebration at the end of a life. The items
include coffins, urns, clothing and accessories.

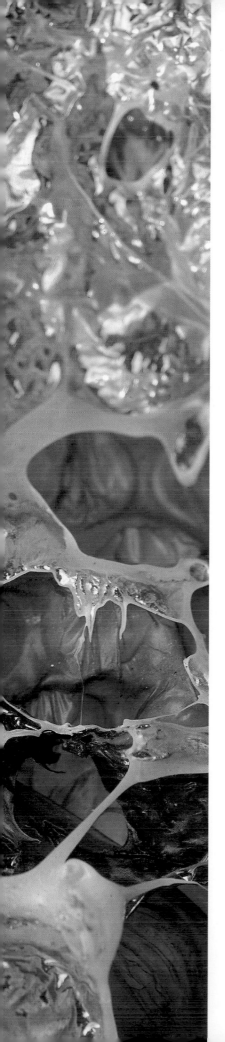

Featured artists

Alison Hermon
Website: www.alisonhermon.co.uk
Jayne Routley
Website: www.ladylazarus.co.uk
Lynn Leese
Email: lyn_leese@hotmail.com
Sue Davies
Email: suedavies173@hotmail.com
Carrie Donohoe
Email: carriedonohoe@hotmail.co.uk

Lee Brown
Website: www.leebrowndesigns.co.uk
Jae Maries
Website: www.jaemaries.com
Angie Hughes
Tel: 01531 633100
Email: info@ledburyartplace.com
Website: www.ledburyartplace.com

Wendy Dolan
Tel: 01273 417178
Email: wendy.dolan@ntlworld.com
Website: www.wendydolan.co.uk
Kim Thittichai
Website: www.kimthittichai.com
Sally Colledge, Sarah Hawkins, Hazel
Ranger, Jan Eldridge, Ruth Hodge and
Annie Kemp can be contacted via Kim
at www.kimthittichai.com

Further Reading

Magazines

World of Embroidery: www.embroidery.embroiderersguild.com
Selvedge www.selvedge.org
Crafts Magazine: www.craftscouncil.org.uk/crafts
The Textile Directory: www.thetextiledirectory.com
Workshop on the Web: www.workshopontheweb.com
Stitch: www.embroiderersguild.com/stitch

Books

Jan Beaney and Jean Littlejohn, *A Complete Guide to Creative Embroidery,* Batsford, 1997

Jan Beaney and Jean Littlejohn, *Stitch Magic: Ideas and Interpretation,* Batsford, 2005

Ruth Issett, *Glorious Papers: Techniques for Applying Colour to Paper,* Batsford, 2001

Ruth Issett, *Colour on Cloth: Create Stunning Effects with Dye on Fabric,* Batsford, 2004

Kay Greenlees, *Creating Sketchbooks for Embroiderers and Textile Artists,* Batsford 2005

Margaret Beal, *Fusing Fabric: Creative Cutting, Bonding and Mark Making with the Soldering Iron,* Batsford, 2005

Gwen Hedley, *Surfaces for Stitch: Plastics, Film and Fabric,* Batsford, 2004

Carolyn Genders, *Sources of Inspiration: For Ceramics and the Applied Arts,* A&C Black, 2004

Jan Messent, *Design with Pattern,* Madeira Thread (UK) Ltd, 1998

Jan Beaney, *The Art of the Needle: Designing in Fabric and Thread,* Ebury Press, 1988

Karin Jerstorp and Eva Kohlmark, *The Textile Design Book: Understanding and Creating Patterns Using Texture, Shape and Colour,* A&C Black, 1989

Index